beach tracks

# acknowledgments

I would like to acknowledge the following magazines for their publication of my work:

*Freedomways*: American; *pemmican*: The Great American Dream Machine; *The New York Quarterly*: i admit nothing, Mike Gold, John Wayne, man and myth, After Dylan; *poetrymonthly/poetryinternational*: chinese apples, i read three poems, turkey buzzard, twit dibble, dearest, the movies, hosing down the steps, a cafeteria on market street, a birth. A special thanks to Martin Holroyd for also taking my photo, beach tracks, for the magazine, as well as for his support for years; *The Seventh Quarry*: of the depression; *Poetry Salzburg Review*: dear bukowski; *Acumen*: brighteyed woman; *Bloodlotus:* katrina; *Poetry Review*: going north; *Envoi*: I am Chagall, The Myrtle Avenue El; *Mad Poets:* reprint, the movies.

# beach tracks

### rd coleman

NY Books™

The New York Quarterly Foundation, Inc.
New York, New York

NYQ Books™ is an imprint of The New York Quarterly Foundation, Inc.

The New York Quarterly Foundation, Inc.
P. O. Box 2015
Old Chelsea Station
New York, NY 10113

www.nyqbooks.org

First Edition

Set in New Baskerville

Layout and Design by Raymond P. Hammond
Cover: "beach tracks," black and white photograph
        ©2003 rd coleman
Photo of rd coleman: © 2008 Walter Thomson

Library of Congress Control Number: 2010907950

ISBN: 978-1-935520-27-6

# beach tracks

*No one is a poet without a past.*

I dedicate this book to:

Johnnie Del Monte;
The woman in the next building
Who dyed her hair red
looked like Rita Hayworth;
both from 172nd street
My Uncle Miron;
My Uncle Nick;
My Grandmother, who refused
To speak English,
So I never spoke to her.
My Uncle Sasha, who was wronged.
My cousins Zena and Josie,
Who always just loved the boy.
My father and my mother
For much, including what i haven't
Come to grips with yet.
Barry and the Christmas
Mimeo machine. We printed flyers
Asking help to stop Jim Crow
Eddie Kreuter, two Henrys
One the refugee who threw me
Over his shoulder at lunch one day,
And my father called me a coward
For not fighting. The other Henry,
Whose uncle was source of dirty comic books.
(Dagwood's dick was three feet long.)
Mike Vlastis. Jeanie, Jackie Hertz,
Miss Moscowitz, Mrs, Herbst,
Mr. Maleska, Leon Haimes,
Richard Cunningham, Alonzo Meachem,
Moses Mashburn, Clarence Walls
Rhoda, another Jeannie
Bernie Magnus, Michael Wild,

"Baby" Constant, Sammy, Jane Gams
Mike Grosso, Stan Memengakis
Lester, Forbes, Stan, Harvey,
Paul. Sheila Greenberg. Even
Rabbi Polish and the Cantor
I never learned Hebrew from.
The girls who promised to
Show us their stuff in first grade
After we showed ours.
You promised...remember?
Doctors Bonime and Bushelow
Thanks to Norwegians, Greeks,
German Jews, American
Protestants, and Russian
Emigrés, Chigorinsky and Bogart,
Panamanians and American Blacks
And Dominicans, the Polo Grounds
Below the hill from Stitt, and the dogs
Fucking in front of the Catholic Hospital
Across the street.
The St. Rose of Lima Cub Scout Troop.
My first day at college
When I stopped being Richard
And became Dennis.

These are simply the names that came to me as I started to write
this dedication: grammar school names, no high school names,
some from college. I know I've left a few out, but some names
didn't come to me, and some still haven't, though I can see the
people in my mind's eye. The dedication's length might have
grown exponentially, so I had to stop. If I ever publish another
book, perhaps I'll continue, and tell some stories, too.

The book, of course, is also dedicated to the usual suspects.

For those of you who may read this, I hope you are healthy and
can pay your bills. Be cool.

# contents

## part i  70 serpent and other poems

## part ii dream poems

## part iii animal pieces

## part iv:  erratic homilies

# part 1

## serpent and other poems

# AMERICAN

*in memory of Medgar Evers*

Without a mirror
In long sleeves.
My hands behind me
And my pants breaking
On the laces of my shoes,
I am as black as the next man.

An American man
Of tragic country, divided
          and poor
America on the mantelpiece.
Crime with daily meals.
American dust blows me eyeless,
          in anger and pain.

Blood, what color?
Who will shoot me?
What will my mirror say
Here or in Jackson?

He died in his battle with death
He died in his fight for life
But, how has he died?
He has died worse than death
And lost his life in the bargain.

# John Wayne: Man and Myth

I whiffle a book
on the secondhand table.
dust cover depicts a white hatted Duke.
stop to skim: his fighting communists,
evil, and the fbi. why, the Duke,
could kick ass before his first Camel.
after work, the horses watered and fed,
he went home, lowered the shades,
and, yes, unzipped, fully unzipped,
and hung his body in the closet
(jughead's old closet, secretly installed)
where his bodies hang neatly on a pole,
image and ego shimmering provide ambient light.
but, the Duke is gone, like smoke up a chimney
no reflection in any mirror,
not even one American made.

# new york city, 2004

mike gold, 1893-1967: Author, *Jews Without Money*, 1930; columnist, *Daily Worker*, 1933-1967

poor fuckin' mike:
i ask for his first book,
*Jews Without Money*
in a used book store here.
it is the cleanest second
hand book store
i have ever been in.
it may be the cleanest
in the world.
that should have been a clue.

the bookseller, snot to the roots
of his red hair, gets copies in all the time,
he said, "did you look in judaica?"

i wonder if the putz puts marx in
english economists.  mike fights
for communism and an ignorant prig
                    turns him into a yid.

well, it is religious,
schmuck, but the religion
is revolution, the prayer is rebellion.

a story of slums,
of hunger, of poverty,
of jews, yes, but only in the sense
we were there then.

when I was in san
francisco, I ate
lamb chops at his home.
i wasn't eating very
well in those days,
and i was hungry.

17

## the bureaucracy

item 6934.2, subdivision, II,
chapter 9, paragraph 33, lines 3-7
cover that eventuality, sir. there's
nothing more i can say, sir,
or, for that matter, any of us can say,
if covered by our rules and regulations.
nothing to think about. in fact, musing,
thinking and expressing are frowned
upon, and do us no good.
our Rules and Regs, we call it the bible,
is 22, 781 pages long; alphabetized into
32 aspects of questions
and is perfectly reliable. like the sun
in the morning and the moon at night.
yes, you may have received
another answer once, although
we see it as a continuum: it is
modified by statute once each year.
i'm sorry to say, sir, earlier regulations
are archived, not available to the public.
yes, they are classified, and there is no
reason to laugh, i could be ostracized
for bringing attention to myself.
i'm just a clerk, but i'm going out
of my way to help; if you care to press
this issue, here is my supervisor's
telephone number, rule 1212
directs me to offer this to you.
no sir, it won't do any good, but we do
want to be accommodating. no sir,
i can't transfer you. it's against rule 69.

## collateral damage

dropping crumbs
on the breakfast table
moves many as much
as dropping bombs
on non-combatants:
the phrase we use
is collateral damage.
it is a deceit, meant to
protect good people
from noticing
that crumbs bleed.
keeps good people
from getting edgy,
smelling
too much death.
death stinks, you know.
if i say, however,
my innocent child is dead
and give my child a name
the good people
momentarily forget
my child was a crumb.
it was springtime.
now fall.  fall will end.
winter lies ahead.

# The Great American Dream Machine

The camera pans hills,
Undulate, beautiful
Spreading out softly,
Green carpets
Touched with brown,
Valleys and orchards
Rich under California sun,
Offering them to kike spic
Colored wop and mic
Sitting in darkened theaters
Off the gritty sidewalks
Of our own urban landscapes.

And Pancho says:
"Let's went, Cisco,"
They wheel around and went.

Do you remember the Cisco Kid
And his sidekick, Pancho
As they rode among California foothills
Saving the ranches, the women,
Of land grant Spaniards,
(Never called Mexicans,)
From grasping crews of cowboy white men,
Protecting the older thieves from newer ones.

Ooh, Cisco, management goon, despite the snazzy sombrero.
Ooh, Pancho, peasant, don't kiss this man's ass.

## serpent

the plane is flying low,
slowly towards newark,
i am going the other way.
i look up from a book, watch
the silent plane.  i have the feeling
there was no sky before;
in the dream there was no sky.
clouds are wispy and high.
flat as the meadows the bus
is passing, meadows dotted
by storage tanks that look like toys.
i am alone and i feel alone.
i am going to d.c. for a wedding,
travelling through a late summer landscape
of dark green bushes, dark green trees,
and silver tanks of explosive gas.
across the aisle, a woman wears a tattoo
on her left arm, a serpent, whose tail
wraps around her wrist, whose body
widens up her arm, and disappears into
her halter and a sweater.
at the shoulder, the serpent is a female
holding a five tined trident.
bluebirds won't perch there
crows and ravens may.
the sky is now thin and pale blue.

## The Lone Star Cafe

the lone star is long gone.
the bull on the roof was lifted off years ago.
and now the building's gone.
the space is rectangular, protected
by postered up plywood boards;
it is almost elegant this summer afternoon.
the north side of the adjacent building
is exposed, sectioned in white, brown and gray;
looking like an accidental early mondrian.
the windows at back are lit by the sun,
instead of hidden in eternal shade.
the lone star served chilli, southwest beers;
country singers sang on a dinky stage.
i finally accepted a bronze longhorn bull
bent aggressively atop a small building
on lower fifth avenue had as much right
to glower there as me, before passing on.

# the bus passenger

some passengers are looking around.
one woman smiles an embarrassed smile.
she knows she is nosy. this is the now-i'm-caught smile.
all anyone heard was a little dog barking,
not a friendly bark, short and high pitched.
little dogs are often unfriendly and bothersome.
personally, i can do without them.
i look up to locate the source of the barks.
then, an old man coughs and out came the dog.
the old man came in behind me. i'd watched him shuffle
up the aisle and lower himself into a seat.
he wore a wrinkled brown suit, wrinkled too long.
his hair was short, white, so, too, a patch
of patchy white beard. his mouth and cheeks are sunken in,
ex-drunk or an ex-addict, maybe both;
the way he looks, his bells have already tolled.
*definitely, he's been there, he's done that.*
maybe it's simply a cough, not further affliction.

## summer day

*i*
a chinese guy,
a chinese newspaper on his lap,
stares blankly in a meditation,
sits across from me.
down the aisle to my right, a woman is holding up
a cardboard sign stapled to a short stick:
all i can read is: "Jews and Gentiles, Jesus…"
I try to see if she is good looking
but the mexican next to me has his hand up,
scratching his scalp, blocks a clear view.
maybe it's time for her to find god.
she gets off at forty second street,
holds the sign up, twists it around,
offering her luscious jesus to everyone.

i like that she doesn't distinguish
between jews and gentiles, she looks central american,
ecumenical unlike most americans.
in the connecting passageway to the bmt,
two japanese priests in orange robes parade by,
then an absolute fox, also japanese,
some greeks gabbling away, irishmen, tourists,
black folk, straight lookers and gay lookers
coming home from work, or going.
in summer it's hard to tell, puerto ricans,
more tourists; a long haired brazilian playing mozart
on a resonant violin tries to catch the transient crowd.
we move fast down here.  disney may reign above ground,
but the station is ours still.  here's a little round guy
whose t-shirt reads "Jesus is Messiah." jews for jesus brochures
have great cartoons. on the streets, signs read "schneerson, moshiach,"
moshiach means messiah in yiddish, and some hasids believe this.
jesus, of course, for christians, haile selaisse for the rastas,
muhammad, elijah muhammad for others.
new york has messiahs enough for a conga line.

*ii*
at union square, where i've gotten off,
an electric guitarist is laying down one riff over and
over, he is wasted and backed by a catatonic drummer,
and a sour trumpet, a glazed looking trumpeter.
a woman is sketching the trio and a drunk is roaring approval;
a skateboarder is leaping towards the horn player,
i expect one will die, choked or mangled by a dull riff.
just another summer day, but at least it's not L. A.

# chirping

short.  large head looks larger.
hair cropped close to the skull.
were i a boxer, i'd test the jaw.
he is either invulnerable,
or falls heavily, a stone.
…makes a chirping sound.
he may think he is singing,
may think he is a chicken.
his shoulders slope,
they are wide, appear powerful.
handsome in a man.
we are at the end of the car, two seats
on one side of the aisle, four on the other.
he gave away his seat as though he owned it
and moved lithely across the aisle,
so he could be a boxer, could be a panther.
these things are hard to know.
now, he spreads his legs wide,
takes up the two middle seats of the four;
talks to himself, will be late for work.
shirt is clean and pressed,
a dangle of keys on his belt.
he is chirping again.  he goes unchallenged,
many sense the panther in him.
his boots, tan timberlands, are new.

## the list

i'm scanning the list:
a bombardier
setting his sights.
the one bombardier
i know anything about,
missed his targets,
regularly,
what he constantly said.
means he killed people
farther from
government approved kills.
not much to brag about:
a moral question
that burrows: a louse,
near the brain,
too far from the heart.
he's like me.
i miss my targets.
the list is my *not list.*
it's all the things i'm not
all the places i missed,
though i aimed there.
keep in an accordion file.
room for expansion.
i expect the file to grow.

# falling through the cracks

butch is probably dead.
if he is, he lived too long
in the minds of many.
he assaulted, he murdered once,
in a bodega: asked to put a beer back.
put men in hospitals,
ruined again already ruined lives.
he was called butch,
butch, a black golem,
brought to earth to rage.
abandoned by his mother.
in the projects, roy and fay,
two social workers,
had the touch,
no one else, ever.
he looked like a fireplug.
twisted, almost torn off
the sidewalk.
fear butch.
butch's eyes are stones.
don't look.
no mental institution keeps him.
given meds like candy,
doped into docility,
set loose, under the law.
no longer a threat to others.
the law, they say.
the jails don't keep him,
the law, they say.
he beats guards up;
they beat him.
returning to the streets,
the men's shelter kept him.

the mad stay away.
bodega owners let him steal.
city, cops, psychiatric workers,
doctors, psychiatrists, social workers,
god, where are you,
butch has fallen through the cracks!

## as i was going to st. ives

it is saturday morning.  early.
i have seven fifteen,
but that's not the real time.
the real time is like boobs
under bras under tight shirts,
may be a flim flam; may not exist;
suggests before coming out,
knows pitfalls back to creation.
that girl over there, the biker,
wearing black tights, biker's pants,
a multi-colored helmet is hung
on the handlebars of the bike:
her time is different from mine
she can't wait to ride;
or that spanish dude, looks tired
already, knowing what twelve hours
of work will feel like: his bells will toll
and toll.  his wages will stay low.
he'll get drunk tonight,
sing songs from back home
with compadres.  his time is work,
his work is eternal.
and that old man, barely five feet,
his hands are a clue to his time
saying he was a working man.
ropey still looking strong,
bigger, in their way, than five feet tall.
i make him for a buddhist now,
he is calm: preparing to go
to the end of the line; the only one
paying no attention to time.
i'd like to see him again.

# blues for our mr. charlie

in the shade, sitting on the edge of the bench,
harmonica's wired to rest against his mouth
he plays a raggedy old guitar,
loses a string, replaces it.  no hurry.
he excites the children going by
the littlest ones stop and dance.
older ones, not real old, stand and stare.
nannies and mamas seem to think he's cute.
don't recognize the pied piper,
bench is right off the 79th and fifth entrance.
he seems to know the deal.
an older couple photographs him,
politely, throw a bill into his guitar case
the park is quiet, except for birds
making their music.  the birds want crumbs.
he wants money; one of the reasons he sings.
his hat is straw brimmed and beat up.
"will not…
                    will not
be worried anymore…"

## washing my ass

after
the morning dump,
I wash my ass.
soap goes
on the heel
of my right hand
and gets rubbed in the crack,
aggressive rubbing
dislodges clotted balls
of toilet paper, pulls
hairs out, and so forth,
and so forth being shit.
if not rinsed thoroughly
the soap burns
like chili peppers
stuck in one's nose,
so i'm careful.
i rinse carefully.
hemorrhoids,
tiny pimples,
the blooming of chilies,
general stickiness,
intimations of garlic,
the past, the present, and the future,
all benefit from rinsing well.
then, I stretch my cheeks
stick a towel up the crack
and sit around, drying
and drinking coffee,
and feel as though i'd
gotten off a bidet.

# piaf

told too young to go see her.
i heard my uncle say, "street...coarse...
no real voice...no discipline...
no training...no musicianship,"
i'd never before heard him
speak poorly of anyone,
let alone a performer;
the orchestra was playing
behind her at the waldorf.

i am listening to radio,
a celebration.  an opening of some sort,
one performer, a european singer,
voice sculpted for upscale cabarets;
a beautiful voice; phrasing intelligent;
timbre on the sexy side of throaty;
she sings piaf songs.  the accompanist is perfect.
no sense she's ever had an empty belly;
her head's in the songs, not her heart,
not *salope,* not alcohol, not drugs,
not cigarettes, not violence,
not the smokiness of a cabaret.
her passion is for singing, not everything,
not life, not the universe:
that is why piaf is piaf.
she receives polite applause, that's proper.
if i had been old enough,
i would have gone myself to hear
the vulnerable sparrow, piaf,
                                        piaf.

## says annie dillard

on the toilet
clutching my belly
with one hand,
reading with the other,
when the light
behind me
bursts through the window
wind chasing clouds west
uncovers the sun.
the sky brightens like
an unexpected shout.
and this is the light that
falls on the right hand page

/ of my book/

it makes the language leap.
light becomes a beaker, spilling sun.
instantly, the fabric of the world

/ appears/

here i am, shitting nothing

/ like mother's milk/

nothing anyone cares about.
and the last words before this

/ incandescence/

ends,
as more clouds roll across
the narrow tiny bathroom window
are annie dillard's
*"We don't know what is going on here."*

# The First Coming

*for Thomas Chapin, student, friend, flautist, sax man, composer*

At slightly more than six parsecs out,
Sounds in vacuum are slow,
                             out of synch.
When they heard,
They piped them through the ship.
Soon the captain requested contact.
When approval arrived,
They were ready:  research had been done
The course was plotted.
Names and places to visit were charted.
First, they would visit the man,
Louis or Louie, and the bandleader,
Oliver. in a city called Chicago.
Those cornets, all agreed, were "something else,"
Which they believed a compliment.
Later, they would visit royalty, Duke and Prez
And Sphere Monk.  Sphere, alone of all,
Knew they were coming.
Everyone, then, wanted to follow someone else:
Oscar Brown Jr., Tony Bennett, Joe Williams,
Sarah or Ella or Billie or a man named Mingus.
They listened, their lists grew longer, were cut
                       and revised interminably.
It started, they knew, with music
Stirred by slaves, who felt pain intensely
But were not allowed to express it directly
So their souls sang "the blues,"
And that sound spread like a beneficial virus.

On arrival, they planned to "rub out" polluters,
Who spread harmful viruses, politicians mostly.
Rest, grow toes, "hit" the bars,
Smoke, drink, dance, "getting down"
And listen to music humans called jazz.

35

## twit dibble, dearest

mitsuko lorrine emails me
offering soma tramadol cheap
as well as viagra cializ le... le...
where the subject heading stops.
how cheap, who cares,
or what the letters are that finish le...

on the same day, ama ackart
offered to make my
bigger licentiousness ecba...
that is curious, don't you think?

twit, dearest, my email program
sets spam on a separate page
and its mistakes are very few:
mitsuko, ama, throat, mingwu
squish, lovetta, fagle, and ep schlep,
all loved, but unopened;
for my health and peace of mind

bonne chance, good luck,
all that other treacly muck
creative as you surely are,
i can't hook you up, what would i do,
were there a virus among you;
were my computer to need costly repair.

how good would that be?

## the movies

this is a good place to be,
a favorite place, a favorite time:
an almost empty movie theater
before the first show begins.
the piped music is john lee hooker
singing his piece from the blues brothers,
his voice riding on the dim lights
like cigarette smoke hovering in a nightclub,
                        something gray in the dark.
I don't go to the movies much.  not anymore.
hollywood's empty and violent; its own ghost.
but this is a documentary about a drunk and a poet,
so, i doubt I'll go wrong.

the movie's starting.

## dear bukowski

browsing a website named for you
i find, set vertically, on the far left
of the screen:

*what's new*
*words*
*about*
*contact*
*bukowski*

double click the photo to enlarge.
i comply.  your eyes are closed.
underwood and shadow cling to your chest
as though they are stalking you;
black background, roach in your lips,
striped shirt open at the collar.
posed but dramatic.

so, i'm contacting you.

celine can't be sitting at god's right hand.
great writer but god must have some scruples.
nor are you.  different reason.  would have to have
an olympian sense of humor, used up with job.
you're both in an alley, right?  nowhere near the throne.

how are the libations?
angelenos are into california wines you never heard of.
how are the beers there?  local brews are nudging out
the nationwides, here.  phony names but better beers.

Since you've gone, physicists
have created string theory.
one infinite dimension of string theory
is death. the religious types love that, the rich too,
both will want their own dimension.
tell you what we ought to do. I'll find a physicist;
I'd like you to find a physicist in the lower depths.
who knows, one aspect of death may be life.
the beers, especially the ales, are better than when you left.
and regular scotch is cheaper. everyone's drinking malt.

## of the depression

i return the cap of my ball point pen
to the tip of the pen. i do this without thinking,
the sign of a religious act. i wear my shirts
beyond the natural lives of shirts;
i throw out food, but hesitate and find it hard.

when my mother was of the depression,
growing up in a scraping-by kind of poverty,
my father made money: a musician, he played
for the rich and the very rich who supported

great mansions and drank champagne
throughout the depression; he played in speaks
for the speakeasy rich, played for glittering hollywood
symbols americans flocked to movies to see.

when i have forgotten to cap my pen, ink sometimes
runs into a jacket pocket, a shirt pocket, a back pocket
of my pants, and helpful people point to the stains
and ask me if i know.

i know my mother was a child of the depression.

## bright eyed woman

bright eyed woman
sitting on the station bench
holding a bouquet,
korean deli by their looks,
                    cheap flowers,
wrapped in cheap wrapping:
                           eyes sparkling
revealing their true worth

## subway guitarist

regulars in subway stations
sit in the same spot,
sing the same songs,
perform at the same times
of the day, same days
of the week.  one,
a puerto rican man
plays an acoustic guitar,
sings in spanish,
whistles hauntingly.
i wave my hat;
he waves his hand.
he stops me, occasionally,
speaks to me in spanish
until he remembers
i don't speak his
beloved language
…the police
have hassled his son,
other inequities,
…other subjects.
last time i saw him
he showed me the
hospital band on his wrist,
a blood clot in his leg;
he almost died, he said.
his voice is a sad voice,
a reverberant voice
that breaks as it cries,
producing more sadness still.
but when he whistles,
he becomes a bird, rising,
and free of any cage.

i know he's over seventy;
his hair and mustache
are totally black.  dye.
that must matter to him;
he is, after all, a public man.

## reading rumi

reading rumi on the train.
the acappella crew
comes in the car, singing.
oh, they're gonna
lay their burden down,
down, down
down by the riverside,
and we're not gonna,
no, none of us, no.
no we're not gonna
study war no more.
sweet singers
in four part harmony
i've heard them before.
they're pretty good

# Nigger be Friend

Nigger be friend
Nigger be hey you
Nigger be human
Nigger be enemy
Nigger be my friend
Down be niggers

Nigger mean anything
Niggers mean
Nigger to mean,
Nothin' niggers don't
Want nigger
To mean.
Nigger be
A private word.

Nigger be bein'
A black silk bag
Turn inside out
Find colors galore
Like Joseph's coat

Nigger be dumb
Nigger be young
Nigger even be white boy
Down with niggers
Sometime.

# The Future of the World, part III

The beasts are gathering. Their plates are filled
as soon as they are emptied. They eat ravenously.
Their ships have sailed salt seas and the sweet rivers.
They ally themselves with tides and sail into ports unseen.

By the time they are seen, they are hungry again.

The women who will be raped prepare. Men beat their chests
and prepare. Children are abandoned. A frenzy descends
on the comfortable. The weak are trampled, rushing foolishly
for safe havens. Alley cats scream. dogs howl. Panic becomes.

Fog encompasses the world. It will last for millennia.
Beasts's laughter alone will be heard. Men and women will
Be equal at last, as animals meant for slaughter.
Until the beasts begin to battle among themselves. Die off.

When the animals may revive.

# cityscape

the city's streets
are crowded with people
lemmings in the mornings,
related to roaches afternoons;
in the evenings,
chosen people
roam streets orchestrating noise,
using vehicles' horns,
clanging and whooshing
provide scrims
protecting cities
from quiet,
quiet is a deadly flu.
mindfully, garbage men
keep it away.
so roaches and the lemmings
can rush
for safety morning and evening
to offices or homes,
home or offices,
into trains on to buses,
offices to home, home to offices.
to home.  to offices.

## love poem

i would write a love poem,
of nakedness and ease,
perfumes
mingled heat on hot nights
downtown,
summer nights in the cabin,
children sleeping close by.
moments carrying us into sleep,
moments of other joys.

we looked out for one another.
we looked for one another
we knew where the other
was there was no other.

yes, i thought, the children were our fertile soil.
they were me, you were them.
i was you, you were me.
nothing was more important than coming home

yet despite our intensities
the tide was rushing out
and the ocean receded.
i would like to write a love poem,
but i have forgotten how.

# kunitz arrives and departs

Eating unsalted pistachios,
drinking long hammer ale,
when stanley kunitz sits
in the easy chair, the one
in the corner of my mind
and watches me work.
it's disconcerting having
the round eyed old man
not quite staring, not quite not,
and saying not a thing.
at times, my mind
is a garden of odiferous,
multitudinous flowers,
or a city street, grassy hill,
an ancient tree.
at other times, a darker place
where roses rot, fruit festers,
feelings cry out, thoughts wither;
and that old man watched it all,
and more than all, and still said nothing,
until he left, before i had a chance
to offer him a drink: "the body," he said, "the body,"
as he evaporated from my mind.

## katrina

let me leave in a box,
that old lady said,
sitting in the kitchen
right by the stove
every burner on.
that hurricane was
meant for me,
my family up and
left me here, they knew
it called to me.
...could smell the gas out by the road.
life was done, she said.
she surely meant to die,
she would not leave;
she fought to stay,
we fought to take her away.
tied her to a gurney,
put her in the ambulance.
old lady, no matter what,
we're not allowed to let you die
i'll not soon forget her
hoarse clear cry
as we drove her away:
let me go from my house,
in the box i choose

## hosing down the steps

it is warm today,
too warm
for an early, muggy,
spring day
dampness keeps
odors close.
in front of a row
of brownstones
a woman hoses
down the steps:
the mystical scent
of water arises
from misting spray.
reminds me
of the cold lake,
i came upon once
through brambles.
on the far side, crows
were calling, crying,
palavering among
themselves,
celebrating themselves,
perhaps brownstones and spring.

# executioner's song

i stare
at ann boleyn,
getting on the express:
that same oval face
the same eyes I saw
in that somber painting.
like ann, she wears black,
a designer pea coat,
a black turtleneck shows
over the coat's collar;
she has silver earrings
studded with diamond bits
hanging from a green gem.
she is as regal as ann,
this monday morning.
like Ann's hair, hers
is pulled simply back
and her neck hidden.
i shouldn't continue staring.

# going north

**i**

going north on the west side drive
just before eight thirty a.m.
the police have stopped all south bound traffic
cold. highway patrolmen in leather boots
stand on the roadway. the back-up...I think...
there was an accident, I thought.

**ii**

memory kicks up visions that never have happened,
parades them as real before us; pushes real events
somewhere inside and may never free them again.
I remember not understanding why the cars were held.
southbound, not northbound. I don't remember
the radio on. I always turn it on in the car.
I made the turn to the cross bronx, and then
to the deegan and continued on to my mechanic's.

**iii**

Jarida says he hasn't come in yet,
and that a plane had hit one of the world trade towers.
it was still sounding like an accident; a b-24 once hit
the empire state. of course, it had to be an accident.
the shop is under the el on jerome. and I normally
leave the car, catch a train, change once, and wind up
at my own corner. bronx to manhattan, thirty five
to forty minutes.

**iv**

as I left the shop, a train rumbles by, and by
the time I'm to the station, a cop: no trains running
any longer, she said. I get a standard cop response to why:
orders, I don't know, nothing, nothing. no buses, either.
it's seven or eight miles from bedford park boulevard
to ninety fourth street on the west side of manhattan.
it's hills, it's flats, it's different neighborhoods. I start to walk.

53

**v**

I bum my first cigarette in two years off a workman
at lehman college, a tasteless double filter piece of string I soon stubbed
out. beginning to feel like an automaton. unreality is
following behind me, hiding when i turn around. that feeling grows
as I go on. on sedgwick, I pass a con edison truck.
the driver did a hey buddy, he has a tv in there. I go in, see
the tower falling.

**vi**

no accident. the scene is playing over and over and over.
I will see that scene a thousand times. each time it will do the very
same thing to me. the very same thing. i leave the truck.
I reach fordham road via sedgwick;
no longer a hill or a street, but a parking lot. cops are at the bridge.
no vehicular traffic is allowed into manhattan. unreality becomes me.

**vii**

I eased by the police, their lights, their cars. they aren't looking.
drivers on their way into the bronx pull up to ask
and I tell them they can go leave, but they can't get back.
one driver believes me, and turns his suv around,
others continue on. some seem bothered by disruptions to their plans.
inwood valley is dominican now, and the radios were blasting in spanish:
bodegas, repair shops, travel agencies, liquor stores
I could have stopped to ask the latest, but I thought I was dying, too.

**viii**

and I didn't stop, couldn't stop. I had to go on. I had to get home.
I struck up a conversation with some guy walking along side me
but he disappeared in a crowd. no singing in the churches. no bells.
except for the hordes walking against me, coming from downtown,
everything was as it might always have been: busy, busy streets,
busier than usual. but quiet. even the cars clogging broadway.
I passed the hospital. I passed the spot the audubon ballroom used to be.
where malcom died. I thought of jeannie and rhoda, who lived
down the block, thirteen when I was thirteen.

**ix**

at the trinity cemeteries, on one fifty fifth
the first bus came slowly by.
I may have looked dead; the driver stopped the bus;
he refused to take fares. we rode,
the doors open, anyone who wanted on got on.
I rode the bus to one hundred tenth,
where it turned east and I walked south.
on ninety ninth, i stopped for take out. it was no good.
I drank. the tv was on.

**x**

by the time I got home, it had all been done. two planes.
two towers. the dead uncounted. the dust rolling towards
all. the towers down.
it played over and over again.

**xi**

over and over again.

# halley's comet

halley's comet
no longer much of a mystery
barreling closer
halley's comet,
a burning icy ball
frightening some,
just as anxious thousands
were thousands of years ago.
it never crashed.
did it pass before
the mountains rose,
reptiles crawled
did ancestors of ancestors see it
before knowing how to pray,
when wolves feared
the lions among them.
we know enough now
to believe the comet
will pass us by.

# the bookbag

*for gregory hirsh coleman, my father*

i threw the bookbag,
the heavy leather bookbag,
it held textbooks,
notebooks,
pens and pencils,
drafting tools
in a felt lined box.
i wanted to.  i wanted
to blot out school
the world, all sound
no, that's not true
i clenched it
i swung it
i whirled like a dervish
i wanted to tear out the window
to the street six stories below
but i never let it go.
during the night, my father had died
during the night, in the bedroom
next to mine.  no one wakened me.
my father didn't call to me.
why didn't anyone waken me?
i wanted to go out the window.
night again, to me
at a blinding sunny seven am
in december.  i was fifteen.
my father was dead.

**one**

the rabbi comes, a distant cousin,
comes wearing a satin black coat
and beaver black his hat
his beard signs of black still.
this stranger gives me tefillin
to wrap around my arm
to wrap against my forehead
for morning prayers,
to bind me to god,
in the basement of the synagogue,
where the old men,
mornings, prayed.

you were lied to
distant cousin rabbi,
fervent honest rabbi
my father died
two days before the funeral.
the family
feared you will not come
if the burial is later than
the day after death,
deviating from religious law.

i volunteer to telephone
all the relatives, his friends,
my mother's friends.
i told them all my father is dead,
my father is dead.  i called them
all to tell them all
what i could not believe.
my father is dead...my father is dead
the funeral is...i never said,
as i slept he died.

never saying at seven am
i saw it in their eyes
they were waiting for me
the eyes were waiting for me
in the living room, waiting for me;
my aunt, uncle, my mother, waiting for me,
his bed already empty
no goodbye, no goodbye
heaving my heavy bookbag
but never letting go.
i cannot cry, i cannot scream
i stumbled torn back down the hall
to wake my younger brother.

uncle emil called the rabbi.

**two**

i put on the tefillin, take my prayer shawl,
the hebrew prayer book the rabbi gives me
                              but i don't read hebrew
and go to morning services
i sit among the old men lost in reveries.
and i never go again.

**three**

headstrong old man,
sick then,
flattened a young man
with a right hook
pulling an old jew's beard.

**four**

i never cried then.

## chinese apples

what he called chinese apples
were pomegranates elsewhere.

she heard the throaty coos of pigeons
others called those coos the coos of doves

both knew not all flowers were roses
but had still no other names, not then.

neither knew innocence became them.
neither knew eternity was fleeting.

## turkey buzzard

turkey buzzard's mocking me,
a stranger, minding my own business,
with its loud and throaty,
harsh unfriendly squawks.
he's hiding in the old growth pines
that run up the side, crown
and crest of this stubby mountain;
i am east of the crest and down some,
sitting, reading in the sun, half asleep,
lulled by sun and a book of poems,
and those buzzard and woodpecker sounds...
flaps now out of the pines, and circles above,
wings outstretched in silent glide.
hard to see the fierce or nosy him, or her,
like those fighters hiding from the enemy
by roaring out of the sun.
no, brave pilot, no confluence
of events will get you me, today.

## nynyny

heavy bones, high cheekbone,
high brow, sculpted lips,
a handsome man
chanting from the far end
of the subway car: "Roses! Roses! Roses!"
after each word, he pauses
allowing their enormity
to sink into our souls.
he holds single roses,
each wrapped in clear plastic.
then he chants: "New York!"
two beats.
"New York!" two beat pause.
"New York!" slow call, as though needy
"New! York!" fast, like the city itself
low "New! York!" then louder.
unclear if he is dangerous.
clear he is desperate.
he long legs the length of the car
to where i am sitting, turns his back
on me and sags at the knees.
the roses dip towards the floor.
he starts a sad dance
to music only he hears,
the subway clatters.
the world is present around him.
he steps on my shoe.
"Mama," he turns to the woman
across the aisle "Mama, I love you, Mama."
she is disgusted and angry,
handsome that black man, brought low.
she stares straight at him.
it looks like hate.

he turns to me, slips to his knees
and rubs my shoe. "I'm sorry,"
repeating, "I'm sorry, I'm sorry."
he cries "New York." gets off at 59th,
doing the heroin shuffle
on the platform, as the local pulls off.

# Notes on the Voyager Mission, 1977

*Blind Willie Johnson, 1902-1947, born, Marlin, Texas.*
*Chuck Berry, 1929-present, born, St. Louis, Missouri*
*Carl Sagan, 1934-1996, born Brooklyn, New York*

*"Voyager takes human music out of this world"*
*"Carl Sagan Sends Americans Out To Space"*
*Carl Sagan convinces NASA scientists to send a golden record on Voyager*


Lord, it's time to get back to the source
drag it back, into our lakes and mirrors
so it's there when we sneak a look,
so it rises up to shuffle, moan, shimmy 'front of us.

As far as hearin' goes, it's nothing other
than the slide guitar, that shaky sound,
it's the hum, his hum, some call vibrato.
It's Blind Willie Johnson doin' "Dark was the Night"

You, Chet, you Miles, you Billie, you Bessie…Django,
we'll bop and be respectful…
But, right's right and out there, Blind Willie, Chuck Berry
and Louie blowing "Melancholy Blues,"
represent us, all humanity.  How cool.

Right about now, Johnny B. Goode may
be tippin' his hat to Pluto, causin' Alpha Centauri
to, you know, shake, rattle and roll.  Here we are, Universe, us!
Backward, backward, backward, ass backward us!

Berry and Johnson.  Sounds like a Vaudeville team.
We'll tell ya' 'bout softshoe and Vaudeville another time.

Meanwhile, go on and twinkle, little star.

## letter to a woman:  from university to seventh avenue

to the woman who rolls her baby's stroller on two back wheels
on twelfth street, passing me on the way to fifth avenue,
whom I catch up with at the red light,

                            as you wait for it to change.

between fifth and sixth avenues, you roll that stroller like a skateboard
champ, famously, on its back double wheels, and again I catch up.
the light again, against you on sixth.

on the way to seventh you fall behind, couldn't pass me.
the sidewalk narrows at the brownstones,
bricked up front yards on one side, trees
lining the sidewalk next at the curb.

I purposely slow down and move to the side as soon as
the james beard house restores the sidewalk's width.
you pass me again.  but, stop, lower the stroller to four wheels
and continue on.  I have come to believe
the tilt made the kid sleep.  a trick, right, based on love:
now, you've decided he will sleep until you get home, perhaps longer.

as you pass me that third time, I feel...love

to you I send my regards.

# S. Klein's Department Store

S. Klein's was meant for the people,
on the north side of fourteenth,
at Union Square, across from where,
everyone agrees, the Lower East Side
ends or begins.

For all the buys throughout the store,
the basement sold the real bargains:
its large tables and narrow aisles
were piled with shirts, pants, blouses,
pairs of shoes tied by their laces,
winter clothes and summer clothes:
an everything place of flotsam and jetsam
washed up on waiting tables.

Old women in black, like in the old country,
touching piece after piece, testing blouse
after blouse, pulling at stitches, feeling fabrics,
vultures pecking for morsels among bones.

young orthodox women, modestly dressed,
slightly lighter colors, ill fitting wigs,
working with one hand, a baby on their hips,
practicing to become older, better shoppers.

the unmarrieds are wenches dressed in many colors,
chewing gum, laughing, chatting, sneaking a smoke.
sooner or later, they will get knocked up, get married,
some will go on welfare, most will work all their lives,
live in the tenements, a few will move to Parkchester
or Stuyvesant Town, where there are trees,
and you had to have carpeting;
now, just wanting to enhance their youth,

which some know how to do,
while some will still be learning.
they all know it won't last; know they won't last,
but a nice looking blouse is for saturday night,
well, that's worth something!

no haggling here, this is uptown,
to haggle, go to Orchard Street.

# dodge, desoto, plymouth

i
remember that indian's face,
his hair flowing back,
with my father's regal nose.
what if i had known
the desoto would cease to be?

ii
it was a maroon chrysler new yorker,
cheapest of the line, but with overdrive,
on that last trip, the one to florida.
the back seat seemed a private acre
for my brother and me.

we drove through philadelphia,
drove past white stoops in baltimore,
smelled the red clay of georgia,
burnt and moldering,
i didn't know adamah is red dirt,
and adam is its human name,
tasted an orange juice
at a roadside stand entering florida,
a sweetness i remember.

that was the summer of his illness beginning.

before that, the plymouth coupe.
two doors, a bench seat for two,
a bench behind, above, next to
the rear window, wide enough for us to fit.
trips, in those days, were always long.
route seventeen led to a different world.
with the roadside rest the halfway point,

we almost always stopped
for hot dogs and real french fries.

uncle nick had a plymouth with a rumble seat
sitting back there was like flying in a biplane,
in the open, free.  i was never allowed to be alone.

### iii
i got caught cursing,
i was sitting on the left front fender
of our plymouth.
my father came up from behind me,
cursing is fun unless you're caught.
i wasn't allowed out to play for three days.
that plymouth had a trunk so deep,
all the kids crowded in, held the lid up,
and traveled to the swimming hole in style.

i don't remember swimming
in the swimming hole,
it was too small.  we caught tadpoles.

what if i had known?
what would that have stopped?
not death or the desoto disappearing,
or trips in cars that now are memories:
certainly not cursing on left front fenders
knowing my dad was there would
just have put it off.

# Nine Lives, Seven Veils

**i**
I am alone,
sitting on the couch,
when she comes,
as she often does
comes to stare,
like one searching.
She arches her ruffling back,
claws at the rug, tensing,
leaps smooth and wary
to the couch, then on to me.

Staring unabated,
she picks at my robe with a
delicacy she sometimes shows;
deciding when to settle, where.
stretching out, staring still,
crossing her regal right foreleg
over her regal left:
her visage immobile, full of reproach.

*Tell me whom I am.*
*Tell me who I am.*
*Remember if you can!*

I scratch between her ears,
in submission, hoping
she will purr, become catlike again,
this female, furred and spiteful.

*My cat!*
*Did you tempt me;*
*Did I refuse?*

**ii**
A cranky comfortable married man
seated on his sofa late at night.
some tremor has awakened her;
she is jealous for I am forgetful.

# The Yellow Chair

The breeze wants to scatter
The chips off my lap,
Into the grass, across the yard.

She sweeps down, over my left shoulder,
As though she were a goddess:
Her playthings, the chips, the day, the river,
The treetops, earth, me.

And like a god, careless: a bottle of McNeil's
Bitter beer remains standing
By my chair, the yellow chair I'm sunning,
Reading in.

Yellow chair and sun…potato chips and ale.
Troilus and Cressida…Hitler and Jews,
Breeze and what it knows.

She assists chimes in playing complex melodies,
But disregards their song.
She sneaks behind me, and snatches at the chips.

I'm less trusting these days, so, so far, i'm faster.
It won't last, sitting in the yellow chair, thinking
Of the first Miriam, the woman I met at the co-op,
Then the second Miriam of campus theater,
Then third, the biblical Miriam, an angry sister, a jealous seer.

If i sit here too long, thinking of them,
It will be breeze's advantage,
And she will grab me along with the chips.

# eighteenth street subway station, irt

it's a gray place, concrete bare,
like most stations on the line.
catacombs are more welcome.
a shooting recently occurred
on this platform, got a moment
on television news: allegedly,
two young men fought over a woman.
what was it really?  blood running
over the barest of facts.
the dead man's father, angry and grieving,
provided a good sound bite.

other murders have been committed
in the city since then; murders are
as natural as mushrooms after rain,
so are world crises, weather reports,
movie and restaurant reviews;
but nothing more about the young man
murdered at my station, where i get off regularly
to walk two blocks to the darkroom.

you know what, i'll forget him.
in a small town, i'd hear more first.
the local news here isn't as rich.

as it is, i didn't get his name.

# Going to BPJ

I have been browsing the internet.
I am in the kitchen on the laptop;
using the wireless set-up.
My wife is a psycho-therapist,
her office is in the apartment;
the desktop is in the living room
through the waiting room space
when she is in session. I imagine
the therapist as High Priestess, draped in black,
wearing a headdress that suits the mood
perceived to be the patient's need.
A kind of intuitive legerdemain;
kitchen, dining room and maid's room
can be shut off from the rest of the apartment.
(No maid, she left earlier in the century.)

I find an old bookmark for BPJ, find directions
to a poem by W. C. Williams: "The Drunkard."
He calls it an offering to his mother. Father? Himself? Her?
Curious, suited perhaps for analysis. I like the poem.
Drunkard is an archaic word, reminding me of an
archaic man. He wore a dark blue bowler hat,
always wore a white shirt with a bow tie. I see him now,
staggering into his cubicle in a bowery hotel.
He is a black gentleman, up from the South, needing the Muni.
He is too gentle and fine to make it here. From Williams,
I go to David Rafael Wang, on page eighteen. Great name.
Two translations of poems I know from Rexroth and Bynner.
Li Po's been a buddy of mine for years.

Damn. I've just bounced. But, I scroll back.
At the age I was instructed to scrub behind my ears,
and still listened, scrolls were in synagogues,
made of parchment, weren't verbs. Now I scroll as handily
as a ten year old...R. Mayes, Tom McAfee. Judson Crew...
I scroll, squint, read, sucked in to this metaphysical vortex.
It's fall outside; hard rain is smacking against the window panes;
it is damp and cold and the Northeast is flooding;
my presence on earth feels improvised.

Today is Yom Kippur: to cleanse myself of sins against God
I would have to fast 364 days. Double that for sins against man.
I offer this light bit of guilt to my daughter, she snorts.
That pisses me off. I really believe it is immoral to wash
away sins. Nothing left for hypocrites to harp on or carp about.
It may just be nothing is left. I'm looking forward to sundown.
I made my personal version of pork and beans last night,
four types of beans, soy, cranberry, fava, and lima,
none dried, all from the green market; fall is the harvest,
always a time to celebrate.

Now I will email this piece to the desktop.
The patients will be gone soon.
Rewriting is a function of the desktop machine.

# radio

**i**
it is five in the morning.
about half an hour ago
I turned on the radio
to  a program the host
called "evening music"
doesn't describe real time;
it's pitch black outside.
working night shift
at the homeless shelter
this was sullen time,
when the dark behind
simple darkness
sucks at you before it dies.

from my window,  I can see
others lit across the street,
exclamation points,
reminders of the lonely hour.
around four in the morning
every organ in the body
begins to shut down,
sniffs at the black hole,
and likes what it smells.

**ii**
at four thirty a.m., i began
listening to spanish composers,
mezzo sopranos, a solo guitarist,
and the orchestra of the canary islands.
I was in bed and warm.

at five in the morning.
i picture the announcer
going to the hat rack,
tilting back a black fedora
so his widow's peak shows,
slipping into a gray twill trench coat
and walking down chambers street,
empty at that hour, not the emptiness
of provo, utah, but the emptiness
of the menace of new york.
first light one half hour away.

# the harlequin costume

the harlequin,
costume-
less, make-up-less,
all that paintedness-
less,
less the wild externality
looks like a common man,
not quite a suit,
cannot hide it all;
he somersaults,
tumbles down streets,
up stairs he finds,
crosses avenues against their lights,
against the attitudes,
the drift of the human tide.
he hangs a skeptical
eyebrow in the air,
stands and raises
both shoes at once,
brushes off heel and sole,
with a brush he has pulled
from a sleight-of-hand hole
in a sleight-of-hand pocket
and returns both feet
to solid ground,
transfixing children
and the aged, too.

# George Washington High School, Tenth Grade

she wore a brown dress befitting her,
as coarse as she, carried a brown bag,
I'm sure she saw dress and bag as hair shirts,
penance for teaching students like us.
by normal standards, not really normal:
el diablo, the dwarf, led a gang from the valley;
flanked always by tall black grim bodyguards.
they would stop girls on the stairs.
steal from them, feel them up,
rape was whispered once. give that some thought,
dear reader. christian sat up front,
alphabetically out of place, but smelling of urine.
we kept him there for her.
jose pulled out his enormous dick daily
to frighten the girls; but no one had to look.
he giggled as he did, and everyone knew.
she faced the class and never said a word.
billy from inwood was going die in jail,
everyone knew it...the refugees, one greek,
one jewish, had come through the war
but were scared of us. yet legally,
we were students, innocent, inviolate.

she asked if we knew how to brush our teeth,
and when. for months i didn't brush mine;
i meant to bite her where flab loosely
hung from her arm, when I was sufficiently
infected by periodontal disease;
i hoped my germs caused pain. i wanted
to slay the dragon,
become the st. george of george washington high.

# hey, traveler

*andy lewis, 1932-2005*


i hear you're setting
sail again.  well,
you come from
a seafaring people;
it's in your blood.
this time it's a forty-two
footer, pretty, i'm told,
with sails unfurled,
and easy to handle.
a crew of one will do.
i don't imagine
the sea you're setting
out to sail is one of pain
or trouble, of paying bills,
or worrying.
ironic, isn't it:
we leave behind
the lives we've lived
and think of that
as death's proper goal.
i expect the sea
you now sail
will have storms,
but, dawns after storms,
are intense, more beautiful.
i know nothing about death,
except that it is: i believe
you have earned blazing dawns,
your forty-two footer
under full sail

hey, traveler.

# In Memoriam: Stanley Victor Harris, 1937-1972

**i**
Do you know why Auden haunts me so?
He wrote lines drums beat behind,
So great was his heart and the love
He held for all mankind.
"Earth,          receive an
          honoured guest…"
Reminds me tonight of you.

**ii**
*I drove down early Monday,*
*Fog rolled past the car,*
*Seemed like it was going north.*
*Ridge Street was quiet, I parked,*
*Fed the cat, walked to work.*
*Tuesday morning Bucky called.*
*Sunday night, he said,*
*The call came Monday.*
*Stoic Bucky had lost his only son.*

*I might*
*Have seen you jump, I might*
*Have seen you lying on*
*The sidewalk had I come*
*In Sunday night, or fall,*
*That sad distinction*
*Your mother later made.*

*That was the first summer*
*We had the cabin;*
*We wanted to be sure*
*Of our standing*
*Before you came up.*

81

### iii

I have avoided imagining
The jump, thump, closure
It brought.  book, the trigger;
The mind shambled.
Hunched typing till dawn,
A squinting black bear, there,
In that long island city farmhouse,
At the east river's edge…
Working days with the kids in the projects,
Hunched typing till dawn, smoking,
Drinking green bottled ballantine ipa,
Black and bitter coffee, jail behind you,
Refusing to go to another man's war,
Working on "hack," where you spent
Your early years, hackensack,
A book of many days, many pages,
You, in every stop and comma, word,
Feeling, chapter, page.  hunched, you, typing
Till dawn…

Got an interview with an editor.
"A black thomas wolfe" the editor said
And you took the manuscript back.
The sentences rolled along in beauty.
The poetry of it.  i would have said a jersey beckett,
I would have said a hackensack wolfe,
Oh, my friend, oh, my friend…until the book was rejected
By another editor as too poetic, too much of a chance…
After working as a writer does, as a writer should.

**iv**

*Books are men,*
*Men are dreams,*
*Dreams are not to be denied.*

**v**

What did jail do to you?
Even your silence fell silent.

**vi**

*College educated,*
*Masters from Iowa,*
*Conscientious objector,*
*Jailbird,*
*Social worker,*
*Son.*

**vii**

*Up from Louisiana, Bucky,*
*Your father, real artist who worked*
*In the post office. In Louisiana*
*Would go up to white peoples'*
*Houses saying Mr. Harris had*
*Sent him, made you watch*
*As he killed baby mice with a hammer.*

*Cleaned houses for others,*
*Your mother;*
*Only trusted forbes,*
*Not sure she ever trusted me.*

*Had to be tough.*
*Had to be. You weren't,*

*You knew, you hid*
*That shameful weakness*
*Of towering kindness to the kids*
*Behind weak eyes, and the sarcasm*
*A writer has a right to.*

*Nipper knew how human you were.*
*But who knew it else,*
*Before it was too late?*
*And if I had...*

**viii**
Stan the tough guy.  that's when
We met.  *i met a man...*
Tumbling down a flight of stairs.
Stan doesn't like pipe smokers, i heard.
A college crowd, stan instigating
A fight between sammy and paul.
I stood between them,
Got conked on the head.
Came from being shorter than the others,
But willing to go after stan.
Stan was six five.
I was five five.  that's when we met.
Harvey had provided a mythic reputation.
And you, self righteous, like me.

**ix**
*Phantoms started*
*Chasing you, writer,*
*My friend,*
*And found*
*You waiting, willing*
*Blown.*

84

**x**

*Forbes said go out there Denny.*
*You sat in your back yard.*
*We had IPA and Uncle Jack.*
*You told me your editor's girl*
*Wanted to marry you.  She wanted*
*To fuck you first.  We watched*
*The lights of Manhattan. We watched*
*Tugs going up and down the East*
*River.  The police were called when*
*You ran through those quiet streets naked.*
*The cops were good to the madman*
*Took you to Queens General.*
*That was the first time.*

*You had to be tough, too,*
*Brittle, my friend, brittlebear, Stan.*

**xi**

*Forbes and I did our thing.*
*We told the recurring psychiatrists*
*In the recurring hospitals as you*
*Were doped up and let go, genius!*
*Writer! Harmful to himself and others*
*Magic words, they panted to admit you.*
*I lose track of the time, of the years.*

**xii**

Down on ridge you got barbara's
Apartment, around the corner from us.
The kids loved you but were afraid.
Lee, came later, would never have been
Afraid.  turning on to ridge that monday
Morning, your apartment house did not
Scream in pain.

### xiii

*Psychotropics dull mind.*
*Psychotropics dull spirit.*
*You slowly said.*
*Working at the Gold Star Mother,*
*Doctors called that alive.*
*Nothing to look forward to.*
*Did you say that, Stan, or did i hear it in the silence,*
*As we pulled on bottles of ale?*

### xiv

Asked to say words.  i did,
But mostly i looked at faces
People came together
For their together tough guy.

### xv

*Remember, forbes and i*
*Brought that bottle of jack daniels.*
*Put it in with you.*

### xvi

Earth, receive.

## Layla and Majnun Visit the Dom>The Electric Circus>The Community Meeting Halls

*a recollection*

tom and i would sit in an empty meeting room.
keep doors open.  chairs roughly
arranged in a semicircle are in front of us.
tom takes his flute from its cushioned box;
and i open a sacred book to the passages
we chose to perform.
i read and when i paused and nodded,
he improvised melodies, heard never before,
and would never be heard again.

men and women, there for meetings and events,
wander in, sit and listen, and wander out.

as almost all do.

## modern dance

street performances
were once common.
she catches my eye,
no crowd around
her long hair hid her face;
she dances near the curb.
bends fluidly at the knees,
goes lower, is graceful,
then rises as gracefully again;
the long hair falls aside:
his eyes are closed.
he rubs his nose and now his face.
slowly, ecstatically, he begins
to sink again, eyes still closed.
Oh, skinny little man, dance,
your orchestra is better
than the philharmonic,
it plays the music of the spheres.
and he's dancing with her
his sister, his bride, his mother of god,
his queen, heroin.

## After Dylan:

*sitting with her in the White Horse where full fine judybarmaid freely offered house drinks; her glint of eye melting ice, warming all.*

Blowzy, beery, tongue-tied
Bellybusted,
Blessed by candle's eye
The turning tides,
He watched beautiful women
Until his heart hurt,
And the swept tide passed:
His shy tide, his strong tide sweeping past,
Lips of kisses, swells of breasts,
Love's bellybusted dreams.
Beerypinioned, stumbling towards his bed,
Turmoiling through space and time,
Wishing his wantings,
Wanting now to crow and settle in,
To slumber like a soft kettle, fall scalded to sleep,
Scorched by the candle's eye:
Sleeping on tides of veils veiled
dreams undreamed.

## blues for the distant train

hear that
whistle blowing:
going, going,
crying "going, gone,"
crying "going gone,
come along,
come with me."
sorry, lovely sound
in darkness passing,
i cannot come
with you this night,
my work to do.
my life to live,
another night.
we'll know:
that's as close
to promises i can keep:
then you'll be me
and i'll be you,
whistle blowing,
and others will then
hear me.

# brancusi, chagall, traylor

*after seeing a Bill Traylor show at the Studio Museum*

don't sniff, see.
american outsider, so called.
they stickin' labels on everything
american insider, i say
born with a soul in alabama,
worked his soul out in alabama,
moved from country to town in alabama;
not homeless way we know homeless.
poor. lot of people poor.
didn't read or write but signs his name clear.

his people fly.
his animals fly.
his flowers fly.
his birds fly.
his people drink.
his people point.
forms not just abstract:
forms human
and abstract,
so i think.

somewhere i read he didn't read write
only spoke english, but. seems an insult.
spoke art.

## Baghdad

old woman says
old as she is, she says
should not be forced
through the streets
nightgowned,

running.

## stein and picasso

after a while, she liked
her hair short.
as evening ended,
picasso decided
he, too,
liked her hair short.
they agreed, however,
the portrait
defined her,
not the current style:
wrapped long hair
looped in a roll on top.
and clearly definitive
of her, in an eternal
sort of way

## How Sweet I Am

"How Sweet I...I...I Yaaam,"
shabby man in gray yells out
to no one in particular.

maybe he's seventy, maybe older.
a whale, listing along,
a voice of pebbles and spit.

says he loves himself,
but wrists and hands gesture
erratically, as though in debate.

he loves himself, he says.
I hope he does.  loving himself
does make it sweeter.

## not even in america

she stands, staring off into space.
she has put laundry in the machine,
but her machine doesn't run.
I am folding my clothes.

"I forgot the soap, she says,"
to me and to herself,
"the soap and the quarters."
she laughs, she blushes, she smiles.

"i do that, too," i say,
"who remembers everything?"
she laughs and smiles.
she knows it is old age,
knows no medicine protects
her from disappearing life.

she lives in the building,
many here ran from europe
in order to stay alive.  her husband is gone.
I still see her, walking up the hill,
for a newspaper, or to the grocery,
getting smaller, slower, still determined.

# mournful poem

false dawn fooled me.
last night, wind blew hard
against the window
and through the screen,
an angry presence,
the shade flapped,
a wounded bird,
the door knob rattled,
like someone locked out.
gray the dawn, the false dawn
is going to end.
awakening came with surf
rushing across a gritty shore,
softening up the beach,
fleeing rushing back again.
sleep was my ocean;
quiet was my dream
and everyone sleeping;
a quiet filled with light.
i arose with an ocean,
sat, bedside, naked, alone,
as real dawn appeared.

# the clock reads seven a.m.


a single family house.  a wrap around porch.
i am looking at it from the rear.
a dim bulb is on in the back room;
steam billows from a pipe.
snow appears pristine in this back yard,
bush branches are bare, dark metal cut-out
designs are nailed to weathered wooden
fences, grayed by massachusetts weather,
the glow of the early sun lights the eastern sky.

the second day.  day.  the clock says 7 a.m. yesterday,
a child was born.  it is march, but at 5:10 pm, yesterday,
it was still winter dark in his town, one town from watertown,
where i am now.  i am seeing, thinking of nothing,
which means, of the world of the ways of the world,
of a child born into this world; of everything,
which at times is like nothing.  i am looking out at the quiet snow
and noiseless steam; his mother is my daughter.
she is well and the child is well.

i see the outlines of a man under the dim bulb
from the room where the steam seems to come
and i thank him without his knowing it.
he must see me, standing as i am at large windows
facing east, meant to receive the morning sun.
dusk removes day, just as dawn brings it.
and now the world is filled with promise; lives advance
on multitudes of promises, difficult as they are.
my lovely grandson will see it all some day.

# Searching for Clark Kent

*I had a dream last night,* my mother says;
She is hospitalized for a staph infection
resulting from cataract surgery.
She's is eighty three.

*They were looking for Clark Kent.*

Who's they, mom?

*Harriet, your Aunt, you know her
don't you, and me. We're they.*

I've know Harriet all my life
but I don't say anything.

*She schlepped me all over Harlem.
She was wild about Clark Kent.
But we couldn't find him. We were kids then.
We lived on one hundred and seventy eighth street.
Lots of people. The bridge was just opened.
Did I say she schlepped me all over Harlem?*

The Bridge opened in 1930 or 1932, mom.
Didn't you live in the East Bronx then?

*We lived in Highbridge. It was a footbridge
going over the Harlem river...*She is adamant,
I've never heard a Highbridge story.

*...She was wild about him.
This was real and I dreamt it, too.*

*We were looking for him and we went into bars,*
*and we went into stores asking for him.  And, I think*
*we finally found him.  Harriet was wild about him,*
*but he was older.  He must have seen her as a kid.*

How old were you, ma?

*Twelve maybe.  Maybe fourteen.  Did I say we went*
*                                    into bars and stores?*

You and Harriet really looked.
What's his name again?

*Yes! Oh, Clark Kent is the other one.*
*Maybe his name was Kent.  Just Kent.*

Its been a while, mom.
Maybe his name was Clark Kent.

# i can only write about the city

late into night, morning soon
the moon has moved above my window,
high always, it illuminates the rear
of the building at this hour. i have to move
to the window to see it.
the moonlight never makes a sound.
even the streets have quieted.
a yell from a drunk to his friends,
a truck lumbering down broadway,
a car that whooshes, occasionally a bus puffing.
the trees in the central mall lost leaves
weeks ago, and the hard wind through the branches
barely moves them. the wind is banging
against the windows.

# of cabbages and kings

wang wei is sixty
and he dies.
walt whitman is seventy three
and he dies.
raymond carver is fifty
and he dies.
kenneth rexroth is eighty three
and he dies.
pierre ronsard is sixty one
and he dies.
william blake is seventy
and he dies.
their works don't.  won't.
there are cabbages,
princes and princesses,
queens and mountain men,
and there are kings.

## squat toilets


we return from chartres
in the borrowed fiat.

this is our first trip
to the continent, the first
to paris, the first without children
in seven years married.
three children now,
one more will be adopted,
if we leave the lower east side.
the agency says
we need a larger apartment
that means, not in a slum.
at a red light along the seine,
a passenger in the next car over
reads a newspaper
the headline: Nixon Réélu!
we are glad to be here.

we take a bus from Orly,
passing a Rodin
in a neighborhood park.
oh, paris. yes.

faye disapproves of the hotel
we booked, friend recommended.
i drag luggage across pont de la concorde.
there is notre dame and the louvre.
i haven't slept for a day and a half
but i'm dragging luggage across the seine.
the travel agent offers a right bank hotel.
impossible! after a hassle,
i drag the luggage back again,

this time to rue de bac
corner, rue de l'université:
the bathroom is not in the hallway.
we have both bidet and balcony,
from which we see a small but open
restaurant.

we don't yet know the custom
of closing after lunch,
so we go down, enter.
we are told lunch is over.
in execrable french
i beg madame to serve us:
our first meal in europe,
in  france, in paris,
pity two new yorkers
so tired, so hungry.
we no longer remember
what we ate.

in the morning, the hotel serves coffee and croissants
in its small lobby.  we are thought to be canadians
because we are polite.  after, we choose a direction
and walk, and eat lunch wherever we are.

next to the hotel is le baobab;
a glory to eat with the little prince.

I wear earth boots, denims, a beret;
my wife has a huge afro,
she is the most beautiful woman in paris.

bouillabaisse across from Bon Marche;
morels on chicken near les invalides:
although, the maitre d' seats us in a corner
to keep us out of sight of the bourgeoisie.
privacy is beautiful.  morels, unbelievable!

i use the bidet religiously,
to calm raging hemorrhoids,
that accompanied me on air france.

Here is paris: the bidet, wines, food,
balance the torture
of the squat toilets in bars and cafes.

shit, it is like the sixteenth century.
i plan to stop complaining
and have a drink with Pierre Ronsard.

# i admit nothing

i admit to nothing
my lawyer, an admirable man,
recommends i admit to nothing
my mother, who is dead,
recommends i admit to nothing;
a friend, for whom truth is a breeze,
recommends i admit to nothing.
the moon, her lips sealed
suggests i admit to nothing;
the stars, who squint at me,
when i squint at them
tell me flat out admissions
beyond the proverbial nothing
are cereal bowls of black holes.
the police, picked me up, taped my mouth
and forced me to admit to nothing;
dead relatives sit around the dining room
table, eating cakes, dropping acid
and saccharin into their tea
build the throne for grandma higher,
so she could tell me admit nothing.
my father didn't like the coffee
disapproved of saccharin, disapproved my grades,
disapproved of me, and even he
told me to admit nothing. it was unanimous.
i am writing from an undisclosed location
unhinged, constipated, and i admit nothing.

# it is best to say nothing of vietnam

when hate gushed like oil wells love and peace carried baggage of hate hippie italian girls from bensonhurst put out for black guys. cops hated niggers blacks pissed on cops hippies hated lyndon, hippies hated richard milhouse. hate was purer than weed or heroin. the straights hated druggies and beats and hippies. druggies and beats and hippies hated straights and sometimes fucked 'em up. real folk music was fucked jazz was getting fucked tie dye tie dye tie dye die die die die die die okay to fuck up straights. kent state murders students. okay to beat up blacks and druggies. murdering blacks nothing new blacks getting guns raise the fist raise the tight fist raise the black fist race wars raced. americans hated gooks. don't even know if gooks hated. they had fought for years for their own country. mafiosi waved american flags. blacks hated whitey whitey hated niggers gooks killed americans americans killed gooks bug wagon bug wagon bug wagon war protects fascists kissinger is still alive being richard milhouse's kike didn't phase him. jail him jail him now oh, hear that sucking sound, buys sandals on bleeker street everyone down with hate everyone calls love sex drugs rock and roll america america and more america vietnam really sucked air it is best to say nothing of vietnam out of revolution, created real revolution, created false revolution, created hate revolution burning burning burning, monk no hate gasoline. girl no clothes burning burning running burning it is better not to speak of vietnam. a helluva war, 'nam.

# beach tracks

jones beach is man made.
the dunes between the beach
and the road are man piled.
but there is no way to know it.
the gulls don't seem to care.
the early morning fishermen
coming to water's edge winter
and summer don't seem to care.
the dog walkers and the runners
and the strollers, shoes off,
trousers rolled up, don't seem to care,
surreptitious couples in the dunes,
in dips don't seem to care.
there early, jeeps and garbage vehicles
and the prints of the early runners
are clear and lead east and west
along the beach, yet the beach
feels empty. the ocean is a feast
of sound and salt air, wind and breeze.
crabs are rotting in the sands
and birds come and go at ease.
beach 8 leads east. you can
walk to fire island, where another beach is.

# part ii

# dream poems

# The Myrtle Avenue El

First, I wander in the West Bronx.
Now I am in downtown Brooklyn.
I am looking for the veterinarian
                    To feed my caged bird.
No one helps me find the vet.
I get on the old Myrtle Avenue El
And fool around with the woman
Who sold me the token.  It was her last
                                    token.

# i am Chagall

i am midway between the floor and the ceiling,
floating in my kitchen without wings.
the stove and the refrigerator have switched places,
other than that, the kitchen is my kitchen.  I am Chagall.

towels cover hissing pots.  my wife is brewing medicines
and teas.
the burbling pots are unattended.
i float above them; i feel abandoned.  I am Chagall.

i somersault at the ceiling; i descend like an angel
to land before the stove to turn the burners off.
i stop a conflagration before it starts.  i lose my head;
i am upside down, I am mad heroic Marc Chagall.

no going farther tonight; no floating through the ceiling,
into the inky sky of distant stars.  no hugging stars.
in fact, i am not the hero tonight, Chagall.

## concentration camp

i am in an old barn,
with other pre-pubescent boys and girls.
we climb up slats.
we fight in hay.
we run away and return.
there are shifting alliances.
when we are liberated,
it is hard to leave.

i don't remember any guards.

# Photo op

A wild eyed hairy man kills.
now, like a gobi desert khan,
he sits on a mound of rugs,
in the middle of an empty loft,
his hands on his knees, staring,
caged.

He solves his problem
by committing suicide.
He snuck out, past guards,
and returned with a weapon.

I see it on the front
page of the *Daily News*,
a full page photo of him
stretched out, arms flung out
and legs spread wide
on his mound of rugs
darkened by what has to be
a pool of blood.

He is looking forward to seeing
his photo in the *Daily News*.

# my patched denim jacket

In a barn...once in West Virginia,
...now Virginia...borders change
along with the borders, the rules.

Now a bus station...reminds me of Port Authority.
...with Rahmin or Rahman, unclear,
who disappears...i wander the streets alone.
a man is paying for a porno flim;
not interested...doesn't matter,
i can't have any money
...in some way rules prevent it.

I walk by a motel, don't want to go in,
it is late and i am tired...
but feel the day...can't see the sun...coming.
Rahmin, my friend, never shows,
i cry his names out loud and repeatedly.

A buxom and friendly woman, like b.g,
explains the rules...offers to buy my jacket,
one hundred dollars...my patched denim jacket,
i love it. i sell it to her willingly. Not for the cash,
i want to please her. the cash is more than the jacket is
worth.

# The church

The pope has gone to lunch;
He wore a blue bow tie
And had laurels in his hair.

Recently elected,
In this very church.
This Pope is not Catholic.

We are in the church, waiting.
Maps show where the oil is
Or where the still is hidden.
We don't know which.

Planning is poor.

A woman approaches.
About my father's death
She is the wrong person,
To pass on the information
She passes on.

I cry out loud.
I accept a multi-colored cigarette
From another woman in a pew.
Uncle joseph smoked.  My father smoked.
My mother smoked.  I smoke too.

Someone asks me what I feel,
The Pope's personal shrink,
From Wien, not Rome.

I tell him I think the Pope
Should have a roman psychiatrist.
I say "lonely and loneliness"
In that order.

And wonder if i've passed the test.

# robin hood

*We have acolytes.*

-the four horsemen of the west bronx

**i**

In a meeting hall, we rob the wealthy banqueters.
no one gets hurt; no one dies. we pass boxes along tables
and watches, jewels, and cash, are dropped in,
rings are plentiful. I leave to find the bathroom,
located on another floor. elevator buttons are painted
the same color as the walls. I return and my boys are gone.
the doors of the hall are open wide; the marks are milling
about.

I back away. the vast building is under construction;
studs and rafters and wiring are exposed; a truck ramp runs
up to this floor and I walk down it and out.
hilla is with me; she follows me at a safe distance, I advise her;
to run if it appears I will be arrested. the ramp breaks
the building line into the open. a swarm of blue uniforms are below,
hiding among workmen. from here, blue ants, easily spotted...

**ii**

I am on a dirt road,
a car raises dust
slowly towards me.
two men in the car
facing forward. ministers who can identify me,
they pay no attention.
I think about hiding the fedora
under my jacket. I don't.
I am neither anxious or worried.

## to the supermarket

I drive to the market in my beat-up jalopy,
park in an empty parking lot, where grass is growing
in the cracks between concrete slabs.  carts are scattered,
and uncollected.  some are rusting.

The automatic doors open,
I need almost nothing; I expect to be able
to walk up and down the aisles, and browse;
twice I run into dead ends.
I appear to be the lone shopper
in this cavernous market.
All I find is one red cabbage
in a bin that could hold a hundred.  I want to complain.
the check-out girl is snapping and popping
her chewing gum.  it's clear to me,

With her attitude, she's heard every complaint before.

A farmer's market has appeared in the parking lot.
at one stand, I see a mother and daughter,
much alike, lips sculptured and full,
skin pale, almost translucent, hair is dark,
it is thick, worn long.  I ask for red cabbage.
fresh produce, they say, is produce in season:
red cabbages are out of season.  the season has passed.
they harangue.  they are prepared to repeat themselves.
their hectoring makes me feel guilty.

An old woman now swoops over and chatters at me,
an angry bird…is annoying…becomes more.
I walk away.  she follows me into the desolate parking lot,
she wants to be driven home; she draws closer.
her fingernails are like claws.  her voice drops; she tells me

she's from the caucasus, gives me the town, the street,
and the number. she also says the homeless shelter.
now she hugs me. my father is from odessa, russia, I say.
...her wrinkles are gone. her cheeks are pocked,
but she is young, intense. afterwards, I feel she will try to kill me.
nonetheless, I will drive her...I will drive her home
and try to leave her at the door.

# the lesson

**i**
the child, asks how to spell, "handicapped."
His eyes are distant stars; he smiles.
he is insistent.  where did he hear the word?
I sound out the letter H, ask what sound it is,
he can't answer.  he doesn't know.
I hold up my hand, weave it through the air;
ask him what this is.  he can't answer.
all I can do is spell the word out;
he will have to memorize.
He is not prepared to learn another way.
that is why he asked.
the word has been used about him,
probably by someone he is in awe of.
if taught by rote, he will always be handicapped.
"My, oh my" I say, "what does this word mean?"
i point at him.  without hesitation, he answered, "Me."
"You are a small boy to be such a big word."
He smiles again.  i have been turned into a teacher.

**ii**
Before he appeared, i was necking.
i was rubbing the girl's cunt.
she was rocking against my hand,
i pulsed into my pants
and she moved in rhythm to the pulsing.
couples were together throughout a dark room,
one couple stretched naked on a couch.
they all were going to go to the shrine, a trysting place.
part of school rites.  I wanted to do what
everyone else was doing.

**iii**
It was then that the child appeared.

# the park releases its secrets

...a stretch of prospect park
from the park side of prospect park west.
water in the gutters, reflects sun,
carries green leaves from recent rain.
down the block, the street curves.
means i am close to paradise.

just inside the park,
right at the wall,
a bear is watching me.
the bear is a bear as i am a man.
warily, i watch the bear.
indefatigably, the bear watches man.

bear becomes lion.
lion stares with rheumy eyes.
lion is lion as i am man. if lion is not flesh,
then i am not flesh. i know lion bleeds;
i know i can die.

lion becomes cat, as familiar
to me as i am to her
then cat becomes an animal
unrecognizable
with bat's big ears,
and grooved rows of pointy teeth.
then another animal appears,
and another, all watching me
as i lose track of them
on prospect park west

until i reach the curve of street,
follow it,
and summer returns.

# Miss Muffet's Cigar

I am given a cigar which is flabby.
after lighting it, I throw it away,
as it lands, a fungus bursts out,
twice the size of the cigar.
I thought a snake was crawling out.
Beside me, someone just shrugs,
knowing nothing matters.

# europe

### i  *paris*

I have returned to the hotel,
Looking for the woman who wants
       to buy the florist shop.
I call the hotel the Waldorf, but it cannot be:
this is Paris.  I know…I've just telephoned Parisian friends.
I say I am in town, staying at this hotel.

### ii  *the nightclub*

Not able to remember the names
       of the jazz musicians,
Americans, whom I have met in another dream.
They speak; I do not understand.  My memory is faltering.
I think I know them, but…Just before I met them, I felt lost.

### iii  *waiting room*

I am no longer in the nightclub.  I am sitting in a windowless lounge,
deep carpets, broad leather sofas, comfortable easy chairs,
a mausoleum, passing as an underground lounge.
I am alone until hordes of tourists
shatter the creamy leather silence.  I get up, leaving my coat
and a magazine
       on my chair.
When I return, someone is sitting in my chair.
I ask for my belongings.  He is embarrassed,
defensive and apologetic.  Remains seated.

### iv  *the bar*

I wander into the bar expecting people I know,
searching each face.  Each face is european,
the waiters and the Maitre d' look like Yves Montand
…don't recognize anyone.

No one knows me, either…stare at them
…no one even seems to see me.

v *the musicians again*

…I encounter them in the lobby…
speak to them…incomprehensible again.
I still can't remember their names.
events I should remember.

vi *the front desk*

at the front desk speaking to their leader,
whom I associate with Duke Ellington.
A woman standing to our left,
asking the clerk about her child,
Who was kidnapped or ran away.
she clutches a flyer with the child's description.
the clerk disclaims knowledge.  I lose interest.
                        Exeunt, the woman
who looks like the woman
who wanted to buy the flower shop, short, plump, middle-aged,
Not my Auntie Marie despite the similarities.

vii    *the arrest*

Through the glass ceiling,
we see the soles and heels of shoes
and trousers, jackets and
                            the heads of men,
one of whom, the one under arrest, is moving his feet rapidly,
As though he is playing jumping jacks…
I can't remember its name.  The bandleader calls the game, *Society*.
I know that's wrong, but say nothing.  I don't know what's right.

viii  *the driveway*

I am out of doors with stoned hippies
who nod and smile sitting on a low stone wall of the semicircular driveway.
They are not blocking it.
They are not chanting "Peace".
Quiet, reasonably disheveled, reasonably...
A young  uniformed cop is with them,
His tie is loosened, his cap pushed back.
He quotes Bible and Koran; his gun is smoking.

viiii  *closing the circle*

The same hotel:
woman for the flower shop approaches me.
She must be very rich; she can't find her way.
I offer to guide her.  I've been in and out
of this dream a few times now.
I know the tight circular staircase is dead
in the middle
of the flower shop and leads to the lobby.
Someone disturbs me, or something diverts me;
I decide I don't want to lead her to the stairs,

                              Or to her destination either.

## medieval chinese battle

I leave my house to cross a field.
Trees protect me.  Two enemy soldiers
Hurry, hunched, along a lane leading to the village.
Do I see them or not?  Can they see me?
You can see them, and me, crossing the field.
An old man hums on screen and in the wood;
The humming stops.  They crawl toward us
in the dark.  It is just before the dawn.

We are in our thatched cottages;
I've seen no guards.  I am asleep, a short sword
is alongside.  Everyone else is sleeping too.
I think we are all soldiers.
The director must know.  He's read the script.

The scenes alternate.  The stealthy army/
Our sleeping.  I may be able to prevent the massacre;
But I am not the star.

## the woman


she, whom I see from behind, has no clothes on.
her left arm is raised
at the shoulder:
a mass of changing colors,
blues
                    within whites,
          greens,
   reds,
a gatherings of saints and sinners,
the darker colors in the nakedness.

I try to change the colors by force of will.

## lovely dream

dreams he is asleep
is being prodded…
she is waking him.
her body hard to his.
reluctant, but wakes
strokes her,
moves downward, finds
she shaved her pubic hair.
he is licking her lips,
sucking her ardent clit.

awakened rolls toward her.

## was last in brooklyn

was last in brooklyn...
saw the heights, the slope, the bridge, bed-sty, the ferry...
        had been in school...gone for a walk;
twisty curving streets defeated him.

himself in a bus station...didn't ask directions...
two women were giving away...something to drink,
        ...completely disregarding him.

...to a wooded place: he saw two donkeys.
standing in oozy mud...impossible to near.
donkeys in profile, one close, the other atop a rise.
vague doubter with his teacher sneered and continued to doubt.

...walked down a dirt road...passes an open meadow...
saw a tethered saddled horse, a building with a "Kaufmann" sign,
above the sign, another horse flying through the air.

he wanted to wash his feet...found a water source, pipe and spigot,
        a pressure gauge.
    washed and wiped them clean.
    Nat, the teacher, and Mary come up;
    he wants to ask directions back to school,
    cannot...embarrassed he is still in high school.
    he wants to emphasize he is a senior,
    could not...self-conscious...in brooklyn

# three planes of existence
*3-8-94*

## the crabs

He is on a sandy beach with others,
one of whom is a crab, and he is like the crab,
they are creatures together, communing telepathically.
they scurry together over the wet sand
                              ...and have a goal.
the crab's claw seems to be an elongated eye,
or another creature piggy-back
...nonetheless, he is comfortable in this company,
still in the dark about the goal.

## charles boyer

As soon as he lands,
he feels tired.  he know he is losing it.
very tired.

charles boyer is on a horse,
the horse is on a king sized bed
jumping up and down,
charles boyer is thrown off...
boyer is frightened, but arises.
practice, he thinks, for a scene.

he jumps from a top bunk, a long jump,
it takes months to land,
the sensation is worth the time,
lands on the balls of his feet,
falls over and is up in an instant.
he didn't know how high he really was.

**dwight or roy**

he descends into a huge bedroom
with a gigantic canopied bed,
the bed, the size of the entire room on the previous plane.
he has come through to sleep; he is tired.
the door to his own bedroom is somewhere in this room.
he wears a jacket which was charles boyer's...
                                    ...the jacket fits.
roy rogers, or dwight eisenhower, sits
                              on the canopied bed.
he can't tell who it is, so he decides on carefulness.
his conversation with dwight eisenhower, or roy rogers,
is about their jackets.
he doesn't think either will fit; the shoulders are too wide,
he sees how large they are compared to him.

the conversation flows logically.
roy or dwight try to guess his weight.
his weight is guessed at one twenty,
                              which pleases him
because it is wrong.  it is low.
he thinks one thirty five, one forty,
...says "about twelve pounds more..."
but he know this not to be true,
says "...about one thirty five, a little more"

131

# salvador dali
*february 9, 1995; 6:45 a.m.*


entering an apartment through a back door.
unlocked.  It isn't furnished.
walk through...find the front door ajar.
push it closed...it opens again.

...pay more attention,
put one hand on the knob...one on the door...
make sure it is closed.
meet hard wind from outside...can't keep the door closed.
the top bends backwards.  one of dali's clocks.
stop pushing...let go...the door is ajar...wind stops.

why doesn't dali want the door closed?

see that the lock on the door has been removed.
...shape of the template... a triangle and half-moon,
on the door where the lock once was.

look carefully out, see officers standing in the hallway.
                not policemen...military men.
hallway intersected by a wider one, forming a simple cross.
...step out, confused by an aspect of eternity...
on my right...a stairway...at the intersection...
...a desk...should be a doorman there...isn't that right
but no one is
...no one.

# indecision

*september 2, 1996; 12:25 a.m.*


I am planning to visit friends in Brooklyn.
when I arrive at the bridge bus stop,
there are buses everywhere.
I don't know which bus to take.
I am wearing only a T shirt and shorts
it is cold and about to rain.
black clouds are roiling, hissing like alleycats.
I am feeling exposed and lost
I decide to get on any bus.

I find myself in bleachers, overlooking a sea wall
facing a choppy ocean, a darkening sky.
whales swim over, dance like dolphins,
their mouths forming hugh O's, swimming
this way aiming for the seats.
dark and sleek and compelling, the O rings of their mouths
make them look like huge worms...I can't move.

# more like two dreams than one
*july twenty second, as well.  11:44 p.m.*


he is being chased,
then squashed...
chased, then squashed...by an enormously fat man.
the game picks up and loses players.
he believes it is a game...but has to run for his life...
to the country and the log cabin.

he observes a man-made lake from above,
made by his father.
something has gone wrong.
mistakes will lead to extinction.
the cabin burns down; the lake dries up.

extinction comes by twirling a keychain, whistling.

## lonely in the dust

in this dusty place in this dry season,
in this Indian village square, a riot begins and ends.

at first, it seems no one is hurt.
soon, I see a woman lying underneath a sheet

on her side, her knees drawn up,
she is lonely in the dust.

two old people enter the now empty square
each from a different archway, each aware;

one is the woman's natural father
the other a holy woman, her spiritual mother,

who spreads a blanket at the foot of the corpse,
                                    and sits facing away;
he sits, staring, facing a different direction.

a mystical wind rises, wild as a gale
buffeting, swirling, menacing, but they hold their places.

until it dies down and the dust settles, the air clears:
and the woman's soul is safe; she is no longer alone.

# the party

In a loft building out of plumb and smelling dank,
A party is going down to which i was invited
By my boss, or my brother, they seem interchangeable now.
I don't belong; everyone here is vague, as though
I am high, or in a dream.

I have an urge to find a toilet.
I won't get to the toilet I saw in the lobby.
told a toilet bowl is in the dim tilting,
narrow hallway.
hiding screens disappear...it is visible...unprotected...
                                    ...embarrassing.

a woman comes and sits right down.
not self-conscious, I really can't see her clearly
I'm not sure if she is dressed or not;
shoulder length light brown hair, her face thin.
men from the party surround her.  she is stuffed in the toilet,
her face bobs up when the men disappear.
I can't use the toilet, now.

the party is ending; it is almost dawn.
I don't want to be the last one out.

in the bedroom with a black man and a black woman;
who may be the maid and the butler,
although there were black guests at the party.
we may speak, we may not.  nothing is ordered.
coats are piled on the bed, but I can't rely on anything.
along with coats, bunches of cash are on the bed
and the dresser.  the cash is wrapped in rubber bands.
it's all over, like lumps of green mold.

At first I think they are mine, I stick my hands deep in my dungarees,
then I think not…maybe the cash came out of my other pair.
do I even have another pair?  my pants are off.
whose money is it?  anyone?  do I get an answer?  anyone?

I stuff cash into my pockets.
I want to get dressed, but need a shirt,
what I see is a woman's blouse…I can't wear it.
a guy was in the bedroom laughing at me, helping me find a shirt.

In the hallway, I hear voices from the elevator shaft.
the elevator door is wide open,
I lean over the shaft, holding on, peer down.
see the elevator descending…a freight,
an open platform…descending by itself:
it should have an operator.  I press the button.
If it comes back at all, and empty,
I will have to run it by myself.
An abiding fear is last one out

## the sacrifice

I am returning to San Francisco.
I intend to stay at the Coronado,
not changed much, except the price of a room.

I am on a plane at the front of coach
broiling burgers and chops.
Everyone, I think, has gotten some.
Afraid there wouldn't be enough...
As it is, everyone is happy,
and the chops have yet to be served.
in danger now of overcooking.
Some are crispy and dark.
Some are white.  One row is lamb,
the other veal.
The broiler itself is open,
I can't see the heat source.
I make sure an old man gets a chop.
The old man is Isaac, his father,
Abraham, has taken an earlier flight.
I am offering Isaac some of the sacrifice.
The chops are a ruse.  I am giving them away free.
I want to be loved by God.
A woman wants to charge...
She insists the price is unreasonably low.

# running

I am running.  I don't know who they are.
I know the danger of discovery is great.
I have agreed to meet with a saviour later.
I ask to rent a tent in a campground.
The proprietor shows me one with an shower.
I will stay here, although they have been here,
And I have been warned they will be returning.
I meant to go to my apartment until the meeting
But it was safer, then.
The proprietor becomes my oldest daughter;
She and I search drawers in a dresser
Shaped like a pyramid, tiers of ascending diminishing
Empty drawers.  I light a Lucky, a mistake.
The smoke is a signal.  My daughter throws up a bedsheet
To protect my identity.  As much of a stranger as I am to her,  she
Was protecting me.
                                    Nowhere is safe.
They are persuasive, powerful.
I want to be myself; they have other things in mind.

# Claudette's living quarters

I am in a workplace new to me.
It's corridors are panelled in dark woods,
Its stairways are wide; its banisters are carved.
The wooden desks I see are massive,
Its hallways are carpeted in deep pile.

My desk is mounted on a platform
Fenced by pickets carefully carved;
It stands at a confluence of corridors.
I see no one; just hired, still feel out of place,
Not sure that won't always be the case.

Searching, I find a room of couches
and easy chairs, probably a lounge
When I return to my own desk,
Chairs on the platform block my way;
On the chairs, rotary phones.
Some with lines that extend into walls,
Others have cut lines dangling from the instruments.
I am offended at the violation of my space,
But cautious, even cowardly; I'm not yet aware.
I return to the lounge for lunch.

The lounge has changed.
I look in and find the room is bare.
The windows have disappeared.
The ceiling lights are dim.
Got away immediately.

The phones are still there.
A secretary, whom I know, is calm;
Her presence is reassuring.
Looks exactly as she did when I last saw her,

About fifteen years ago.
This woman fought for social justice
In her youth.

Another secretary comes along.
She is dark complected,
Speaks rapidly with an accent.
I mention the mystery of the lounge,
And she is full of sympathy.

Then we are in bed together.
I wish I knew her name.
We are fully dressed under blankets.
We begin heavy petting.  She unzips my pants;
I am growing hard,  becoming more and more
Aroused and she is too and we are having
Equal trouble disrobing.

I look away from the bed
To see an open bathroom door.
On the floor are two dolls.
One doll is a diminutive boy.
I mean to ask about the dolls,
But the sex becomes intense
I close my eyes.
My mouth is busy.

I open my eyes, I see dark nipples
That taste like sweet cherries
And  immediately have an orgasm.
I'm embarrassed, again she sympathizes.
I look at the diminutive boy again;
I can't believe what I see.

I'm getting hard again, finish
Stripping off my clothes
And help her with hers.
I shower her vagina with kisses
Before I plunge in.
She is moaning and crying with pleasure,
And so am I.  I now call her Claudette.

This is an L shaped windowless, room.
At the foot of the bed,
Is a calendar written in runes

Across from the bed is still another bathroom.

These are Claudette's living quarters.

## the contribution

I am carrying an empty western saddle
On my back, and four pairs of women's shoes,
One of those, a pair of platform shoes.

I am at poolside for a practice.
A millionaire contributes money;
I don't know why...or what's required...

I must leave, so I kiss her
Everywhere on her neck,
But I can't find the spot she wants.

Frustrated, I ask her to touch the spot
                                    I can't find.

# Cathlene's sister

Cathlene's sister won't give me any rubber bands;
the bartender won't give me rubber bands.
Finally, she does.  Her smile is warm and suspect.
They are on a plastic tray, in a ring box without its cover.
Not as many as I would have liked.  I call them "rubbers."
I know this bar, but no one, until I saw Cathlene's sister,
is familiar.  She is slim, red haired, nice enough,
even though i didn't get enough rubber bands.
Rubbers are hanging on the wall behind the bar,
but I can't ask for them.  I'm prevented.  I need the rubber bands
to wrap the metallic slats of the window blinds.
They must be moved.

As I leave, she calls out a number: 905, which is about 1199.
It is a secret message: the union has sold the membership out.

I'd parked in a desolate area…along a virtually empty street,
one ramshackle tenement still standing, looking for a space…
drove by an auto graveyard, reached by a rutted path
                    that looked like a wagon track.

Still looking for the car, I passed a little house
                    and in the window
A man was kneeling, facing front.
Above his right eye, a triangular symbol, brightly painted.
Across his cheeks, diagonal stripes of color.  He is chanting;
he brings his left arm across his body
                    and strikes at something with a doctor's rubber hammer.

Wondering where the car is…

# Angels and Children

My weapons have been taken;
I'm not trusted by these Muslim warriors,
Despite having gained an advantage for them.
I demand a pistol, I am given
A percussion model that fires lead balls.
The advantage is the high ground,
A platform thirty feet above the floor.
I point the pistol at someone below.
Soon the pistol is gone.

Next to our platform, double wooden doors
Open, revealing five musicians,
Two cellos, a viola, and two violins.
Four men and one woman,
They oppose our cause. I alone know that.
I grab a slim machine gun, point and fire, and soapy water
Spurts out the muzzle, gets in their eyes and instruments.
And they run away.

Although it is I who attacked them with soap,
My eyes are blurred; everything is blurry.
One was an angel.
The one with no life in his eyes.

I search now for anything to use as a weapon,
And find a child's slingshot. Small cubes of plastic
Are strewn around the platform. I pick one up,
Launch it towards the enemy below, now infants and children.
The missile strikes an infant, who cries.
Since I have been successful despite the distance,
I launch another missile. This one strikes an older child.

## Dream number 383

the white bugs glow, shine
crawling in unison across the far wall.

a terrific spider arrives
comes from an unseen opening.

and its gone, though it's here,
somewhere, in this large room,

the gathering of bugs is getting away.
the restaurant is likely to open soon.

i go downstairs for insect spray,
get a can from the heavy set man

the upper floor is a platform
no stairs i can see.  i pull myself up

by the railing that runs along an edge.
three women are stretched on the floor.

they appear tired and say they are resting;
we all lie together, exhausted.  one is friendly

another is stand offish, and the third is young
and credulous.  she has large dark innocent eyes.

i am not just lying supine, i am also touching them
the youngest one climbs on top of another,

so i might touch her, too.  she says she is an innocent
and seeks experience; she looks forward to experience.

## aspects

high school book repository. the building is extremely narrow,
grayish, sandwiched between two others made of dark brick.

i am not here to store a book. i am here to store a lamp.
the lamp is fitted into my palm. and glows with a purple light.

i am outside a hospital. i have just received an injection to kill me.
i am comfortable, accepting.

two doctors are with me, one standing in front of me
facing me, the other sitting on the bench alongside.

i have decided the two doctors are one and the same person.
even though one is bald, the other is hairy.

after dutiful silence, I say i regret not knowing them better.
my speech is not slurred, but has begun to slow.

i kneel in the seiza position and die. my corpse cannot
be straightened out. i am allowed to stay in seiza.

there is no place for me at my father's grave site.
i am truly an orphan. i can't live with him in death.

if i can have his body exhumed, to make room for me,
it would be selfish, and completely meaningless.

i cremate myself.

# buying the fish

its face is a woman's face i have seen before…
thrown on a scale it almost slips off.  how much is it
what kind is it.  where head meets body, the meat is white,
the skin is shiny and black,

the fishmonger gives me a price, higher than what i had in mind.
not what was advertised.  do you have porgies, at seven
this was eleven ninety five.

i walk past the bar.  the bouncer has his hand out.
i almost give him a dollar, but he is only gesticulating.
i wait to see the fish; i was led past the bar to a stand filled with ice.

buying for that family.  the parents are poor,
and going home in the morning.
the boy, maybe three or four, is running around with a pocket knife.
he was self contained and very bright.
an uncle is pleasant, is probably retarded.

after meeting the boy, i find him in a corner of a shower room.
I take him out of there.  i am naked.

my father is there, too.  he approves, in some way, of my buying the fish.
I worried over storing it, I don't want it to spoil.

# captive

we are held against our will.
there are no bars, no cells,
only mind control
and nowhere to go.

i have an erection for one of the women,
and everyone laughs at me,
captors and captives alike.
their derision makes sense,
given the situation.

i am surrounded by people
who don't know freedom,
think they are whole,
don't know this is a prison.

laughing at my erection pleases them.

# flight

an old man,
a police chase;
chased to the family farm.
evades, through trickery,
disguised as a black man
disguised with a burka,
bleats like a goat.  even a cop.
enters the hut where he sleeps.
in the morning he will run again.
looking forward to fooling them
once more.

# rasputin

a school gym with tables across the floor,
a stage at one end.  i am at one of the last tables
my back faces the others.

i turn at the sound of applause for M.M.
the entire room stands to applaud.
along with M.M. is a monk.

he is the personal confessor,
a huge man, over six five,
wearing a dirty brown robe;
has brownish hair, stringy,
with a halo of baldness
where a halo belongs.
i moved towards him to greet him.  he towers over me.

closer, i saw how dirty he was.
putting out my hand, he refused to shake it.
he says, "come to me when you have a heart."

his fingernails are long and curved.
i could not have shaken his hand,
not without being gouged.
i had no doubt, either, he enjoys
intimidating men.

# a woman with hooves

I go to a palatial movie house.
The foyer runs the width of the building.
Vast, I can't see either end.
The rug is a rich, dark maroon.
I take some comic books for my sons.
Beyond the foyer, a cavernous room,
No doors, arches framed by columns
It might be one hundred feet across;
Ceiling and walls ornately carved;

I am alone in silence, in emptiness.
Until people begin coming from within,
The movie had ended;
Time for me to take my seat.

Now I am outside walking a dark,
Narrow, tree lined street.
Walking away from the theater.
Behind me, I hear the sound of hooves,
Clear—almost a pounding, yet wrong;
A wrongness of sound,
clip-clopping appropriate to two legs, not four.

A woman possesses them;
Hooves, thick legs without knees
Stilt-like in stiffness,
Appearing grey in the dim light,
And covered with coarse hair.

She wears a dark skirt,
A dark suit jacket, a white blouse,
Wears a hat, with a wide brim.
Sure she is hiding her face.

She had been behind me.
I was now walking past her.
I keep my eyes averted
I am overwhelmed by desire.

As though in response,
She calls out to me
To speak to her.

We are face to face.
She is very pale, her skin is like parchment,
Lips are outlined with bright lipstick.
Black hair is pulled into a tight bun.
Age lines crackle around her eyes and mouth.

Her face reminds me of a prostitute
From a Groz painting,
A whore from a Berlin nightclub
In the Weimar Republic, between the two wars.

I can't remember if she speaks,
Or speaks at all, but she need not.

I was about to go to the movies.
I lie.
Would she like to accompany me.

I don't look at her legs.
She is heavily made up
But i try not to look at her, either.

We start to walk.
I don't know if she is with me,
Or, I am with her.

# part iii

## animals and insects

# cats, kittens, eagles, rabbits

**i**
cats and turtles
seem to have little
in common, though
often share
the same spaces,
and surely arise
from similar
primordial places.

**ii**
looking down
from very high,
the eagle sees
the rabbit;
and rabbit feels
eagle's flight
or dies.

**iii**
not cats
or kittens cute
escape.

# cndiarians

why is a man-o-war portuguese
why isn't it palestinian, or peculiar
to the lakes near pocatello, idaho?
what about jelly fish?  since
i prefer puddings to jellies.
are there are pudding fish extant
among the species?
and are they in flavors, vanilla
chocolate, strawberry, or corn?

oh, cnidaria, o, cnidaria,  i don't
believe you can be eaten or worn.

the family extends to corals,
not sure which side of the family,
and totally inedible, as are
the entire genus, not very smart
and terribly sensitive.
please don't kiss cndiaria,
in roumania, celenterate,
same sting, different lang.
mark this curious gormands,
only one way in, one way out
it's mouth is also its ass.

# fish

orange, a guppie,
a little glass bowl
on one cold night
set carefully down
on the radiator
before sleep.

an orange guppie
a little glass bowl
on one cold night
set carefully down
on a warm radiator
to sleep

# food chain

The diatom, very small,
connects to copepod;
slightly larger, the copepod
connects to sea goosberry
and it, or she, or he
can barely go pottie
before falling to gobie,
who gives up its prospects
to the darling lumpsucker
eating three gobie, de minimus,
at the morning meal.
oh, chain of chomping,
and repetitive squeals,
escalators up and down
make the world revolve.
and now, i ask,
in whose stomach
will lumpsucker's structure
dissolve, lark, lemur, lion,
or jack's?

oh, chain of chomping,
and repetitive squeals,
you make the world revolve!

# his wife first

it is polite
but is it politic
for herbivore
to invite carnivore
to dinner
herbivore knows
carnivore's ways.
what's to be served,
save Herb or the Hostess,
a spouse of many years?

between the appetizer,
the coffee and cannoli,
dinner came politely,
just the same, it came.
the herbivores
are still polite, but fewer.

# Joseph Formica Hymenoptera Gant

I am an ant,
Joseph Formica Hymenoptera Gant,
Or Josephina, whatever's dealt,
Whatever the play,
I am an indoor ant, and small.

I live near a kitchen,
Perhaps in the hall.
I am loyal to my mates
And of course, my Queen,
Who is the sine qua non
Of hymenoptera's song,
Who heads our State,
And promises no surprises.

Ours is a life of hustle.
Unlike ballplayers,
We don't grow fat,
We live on our own
Endeavors, luck,
And within the scope of destiny.

Because a kitchen harbors,
Along with food, an un-humanity.
Please, don't be insulted,
If you sense aspersion
In what I say.
In our scheme of things,
You are the vision

We use to frighten children.
You are the fire, the flood,
The deus ex machina,
Foretelling the spilling of ant blood.

Not speaking for anyone else,
I am a proud ant
And I resent your brutal treatment,
Though, I must admit,
It's the way you treat each other.

Your shadow, you may think,
Drives us to panic: Au contraire,
That Shadow is God,
Wishing us godspeed.
You lose when you bash an ant.

## no escape

for lack of a cat
a screech was lost,
for lack of a screech
a rat was born,
for lack of the cat
that comes with
the screech
the kingdom fell,
the sky collapsed
and no one escaped.

# Sans Garlic

Beware the swells,
Dear stranded snail
And the beach, as well.
Dangers abound on sand.
You, who in some fashion,
Smell and chase the scent of jellyfish
May wind up in a dish
For a lesser animal
Than Mel.

# Sphenodon Panetatus

Oh, Sphenodon Panetatus,
What are you to us,
Or we to you,
Lizard from a land below.
Known as Tuatara,
A mystery you are'a
To everyone but your'a mama,
Except, like homo sapiens,
Your life is eat or be eaten.

# spider

a small black
round speck,
a spider,
is motionless
in the porcelain tub.
with my poor vision,
i barely make it out.
stationary, yes,
but is it alive?
reluctant
to bend close.
not afraid.
i've killed
spiders, killed love.
i won't kill now.
likely to kill again,
spider and me.

## the ants

the queen
sends
legions
to death.
does she call
it glory
or suicide
to venture
onto the kitchen
sideboard, madly
scurrying
across the countertop
running every
way,
except away.
do they see
or sense
or feel or know
a chopping block
is close,
eyes are present,
evil lurks.
do they learn
too late
and die, doing
what the elders
have done,
cutting class when
history is taught.

# the chase

the kitten
perceives
and chases
its perception
across floor
and through open door
into the next room
only to find
herself abandoned
by the perceived.
she remains ready.

## the goose barnacle

a human hunger pales,
compared to freshly hatched
goose barnacles, whose miniscule yolks
make them ravenous
from the moment of their birth,
the same moment they are on their own.

the full blown barnacle,
a bloated chesty fellow,
is the ultimate example
of the consummate devourer:
he summers in the hamptons,
among the riche and nouveau riche.

# The polite locust

Of the entire insect world, we are famous,
A gregarious, a musical sideshow stupendous.
A multicolored magnanimity,
Yellow, pink, and even red, if you please;
And, yes, thank you for the grains and peas.

Schistocerca Gregaria is our latin moniker,
Tho' remembering that can lead to hysteria.
But that's not the reason for our fame:
We are locusts, if you please,
And yes, thank you, for the fruits and leaves.

Cousins are called by scholars, Solitaria,
Acridids almost always overlooked.
Not known, like us, for solidarity;
Quel dommage, never got into history books
We locusts are the boulevardiers, if you please,

Paying homage to gardens, vegetables, and trees.

# part iv

## erratic homilies

apartment fills
emptiness pushes the air out
goes about its business.

∞

it comes slowly
the eighteen wheeler
on a western road.
headlights first.

∞

i answer calls
from strangers
asking for votes.
some are alive
some as good as dead.

∞

a carriage on the royal road
carries the queen,
richard hugo riding with her,
why, richard, why?

∞

those who cling
to a top drip of water
going over the falls
are idealists.

175

the delaware memorial bridge,
a humped back whale,
deciding to swim in every sea.

∞

where appropriate,
i associate nothing
with myself.

∞

our father, come back
i miss thee
come back to our heart
bring heart
the peace it once knew
when you were last here.

∞

"vous comprenez?" she asked.
"rien," in answer
"nichts," i said, and "nein."
"do you understand," i heard
her softly "nothing" me.

∞

a wisp, caught
in another wisp
and another.

poet, sniper,
lies in wait,
for the word
to come.

∞

the upper level of the bus
is exciting.  ask any
three year old.

∞

yellow leaf fallen
children in the sun
yelling after school
storing up for winter.

∞

you are dessert
frothing in warm chocolate
bitter, bittersweet, sweet
of summer plums
and spring strawberries.

∞

one fish two fish
i read the book aloud
add a story about a whale
he begins to eat the book.

don't turn wretched feelings
into law.  if you do
keep them away from children
and dogs.

∞

wind whips rain
rain batters window
wanting in,
frightened, outside.

∞

sky is night
stars tumble
into bed, days.

∞

i turn on the lamp to write.
the bed is uncomfortable.
the city is a few cars passing.

∞

the empire state
is not as commanding
as it once was.

∞

in the dark, i see the dark

man laughs white teeth
holding the other's elbow.

∞

the man in the red sweater
is talking
                    to himself.

∞

one needs madison avenue.
another
                    the back door.
the driver copes.

∞

a cell phone on his ear
his eyes scan
orange cap with brim

∞

white sneakers.
shrunken.  cane's handle
silver.  heavily made up.

∞

the city is
waiting to be peeled
like an onion.

she stares
he stares
their hearts
are beyond
their eyes.

she relaxes.
her eyes are wider.
her lips, apart.
it has passed.

∞

poems are guts.
coral and green
gray and red
guts stink.

∞

i am in trouble
when i repeat this litany:
*flush*
*pick up my pants*
*wash my hands*
*dry my hands*
*check the flush.*
it's not much
but all i have these days.

∞

it is early morning.
she gets on the elevator
says she is tired,
tired and late.  rushes out
of the elevator.

children are not
simple.  i don't care
if you don't know.

∞

my memories
are incomplete.
my fault.

∞

i keep wanting
to think of her
my mind hides
her away.

∞

purple hair walks by me
hurrying.  her blouse,
black and white stripes,
vertical, on her legs, horizontal.

∞

look bored.
absent, not here.
already.
where they are going.

in meditation
time is the lover
disrobing slowly,
               before
entering the beloved.

∞

mother bear and cub
see a hairy man
sitting on a picnic bench,
eating. turn away.
he spoke softly to them.

∞

dogs look into
our eyes.
their sadness
is ours.

∞

i have to beat jet lag.
television keeps me up.
can't drink single malt
lying down.

∞

mind is a mountain
i am on foot
on a scant path.

i see a man
looking into
the distance.

∞

the first shangri-la
was found by a fisherman
sixteen hundred years ago.
that was in china.

∞

bow legged on a bicycle.
straight on a skate board.
a white and blue police car,
lights on, standing.

∞

in an empty bus
in my favorite seat
in mid-morning
in mid-manhattan
at thirty fourth
two people, finally

∞

one half
of a cell phone
conversation.
at seventeen, her daughter
has a baby
and won't accept responsibility.
the mother is behind me.

heavy breasts of a mother
pushing a stroller.
homeless man at his table
hands in pockets, pacing.
two women in tagalog, chatting.
buddha spirit on an autumn street.

∞

the hoards
leaving school each day
are filled with excitement
no matter what they know,
or don't.

∞

boy looks down the tunnel
he is curious.
rub this trait on your forehead.
and don't wash.

∞

jets tear
the sky apart
remnants fall
to earth
like leaves.

a child drinking Ssips
from a cardboard box
with a plastic straw
almost an anagram for piss.
child has the decency
to cough.

∞

at last, a local
not steaming with bodies
as crowded as death camp
trains were said to be.

∞

the two year olds
mimic everyone
they see.  parrots,
they'll grow up.
everyone is smiling.

∞

starbucks, ubiquitous cup
too bitter, black, cloying sweet,
right up ostentatious alley

∞

either closed for good,
or closed for now.
the sign.

i am sucked in
rutabaga's got me
by the ankle, leeks menace.

∞

ubecha ma fa so
ubecha ma fa sai
african, pure poetry.

∞

i read poems
of ancient chinese women
what about those about me,
here in the subway car

∞

he lists a little.
wears sneakers and denims,
as he must have,
years ago.

∞

she carries the baby
in a sling
soon
she'll need a larger sling.

four steep flights down
to the express.  at war.
bombs won't get me.

∞

i knew laughter
as a sign of happiness
would not last.

∞

that old lady needed
to be handed down
getting smaller,
going toward infinity.

∞

there are advantages
            to seeing
what you see

∞

lying in tall grass
blowing smoke
from a hand rolled
towards the sun,
watching it disappear

a
chin falls into the chest
back curves
i am a turtle
shell is my mystery

b
was i turtle
was i man
eye asks
asks
asks the question,
the question again

∞

carry a spade, traveler!

∞

mt st. helens sits behind
the bamiyan buddhas.
natural disasters.

∞

the temperature dropped.
the heat was sent up.
overdressed, yesterday

the drone of the
bus, silence
except for
the essay on
dickinson

∞

i see umbrellas
hurrying down the street.
the traffic sounds like rain.

∞

who is who?

∞

blind show
we need not see
deaf we need not hear
but, o, my fear

∞

venerate thelonius,
the monk.
a better world

eat shit
lots. try not
to smile.

∞

cold
breathe
gray as
the sky

∞

i have been
in second childhood
twice.

∞

open heart
speaks
the first language

∞

minds are sieves
keeping out, letting in

∞

trusting god is error
believing buddha is error
self is error

saw a valley
verdant and hilly
in a dream

∞

i might have
had a chance
to fuck tiresias
had i been there

∞

test dirty
if clean
doesn't work

∞

if you repeat
what you hear
often enough
you go deaf

∞

it writes me.
is there even
a thimbleful
of love
between us?

bach is no slouch.

∞

i began to love
before i had a heart
write, before hands

∞

rhymes
with 'zen'
'vu den?'

∞

not sugar
in tea
cakes and tarts
on the table.

∞

soul plays the flute
i am empty bamboo

∞

i wake from
real dreams
into other dreams

the infant
has to be selfish
she sleeps like a baby.

∞

in the museum
goddess on the goblet
has no nose

∞

old man said:
get caught
if chased by women.

∞

not mine
what a joke
nothing is

∞

more madness
more hilarity
more me

∞

i scratch my ass
wait for thoughts
to come

use a ball peen for pecans

∞

dawn
is often
yesterday

∞

fuck you, i
meant it

∞

if i were a dresser
i would like cedar drawers.

∞

thoughts pigeons flurry crumbs

∞

truth truth truth
comes out of her mouth
like machine gun bullets

∞

honesty honesty honesty
what of it?

wear a woman's coat
not a woman, dressed
in my own bones
not necessarily human.

∞

lost love once
then again.

∞

this business of nothingness
is an invisible mask.

∞

if he never jerked off
he will sit next to god.
better god than me,
tippling in hell
thinking wisdom is shit

∞

basic to the soul
is its
love of malt whiskies

∞

knowing nothing
is a figment
of imagination

mind is a free for all.
i am the donnybrook.

∞

morning sun
embraces me
rubs my face, too

∞

since the towers fell
i cry over little things
it won't stopped.

∞

wake up with a jolt;
i have been there again

∞

pain, the real world,
best to be human

∞

moment
blossom
woman

i am a heap
in a corner
of my mind

∞

in the silent line of the long road
in her
in everything

∞

challenge universe,
the furthest star
the self

∞

in a tavern
in the middle
they flipped a coin
one went west
the other, east

∞

that light
dispels
that darkness

i am the captain
of the boat
taking the dead
to potters field
the convicts
dig the graves
shitting and pissing
in the holes

∞

of all the prides
i have stepped in
race pride hardest
to scrape off

∞

if i told you
what i didn't know
i'd be like everyman

∞

if i told you
what i do know
you'd shit die
laughing

∞

who would suck
my dick
if it reached to heaven?

man standing next to me
between the cars
is dead

∞

beware the undertow,
enlightenment

∞

sitting and meditating
bad habit
luckily, i brake the rules

∞

children are believers
aren't they?

∞

there is no end
to a beginning
where does the end
begin?

∞

i am as narrow minded as they are.
i'll have to get rid of my mind.
will it shrink enough to hang it on the wall?
children will think a shrunken mind is cool.

one thing comes from soul,
another from heart
third from the universe
i think so.

∞

later, i said my father will pay you
or my mother.
when i ran away everyone waved.

∞

they asked if he could move.
when he said no they stole his sled.

∞

jewish meant being, not praying

∞

no past no future

∞

the synagogue is a foreign place.

∞

memories of pogrom in odessa.
sun rising over ur.
you ask what reality is.

"chaa," throated cecil
the sea sick sea serpent,
"iss talking lamppost"…eeeeqew!

∞

only faith can care for me
when i have a cold.

∞

buddha and st. thomas
were celibate. do you think
they masturbated?

∞

open my mind
fear rushes in
eats the maggots, first

∞

fear: a swamp with critters

∞

where did the second self come from, the third…

∞

a universe
a bird passing
high above

the land the reich chancery
stood on was once owned
by jews,  ho ho he he ha ha,
karma, skinheads

∞

close my eyes.
darkness
open my eyes.

∞

my bowels
among
night sounds
fantastic

∞

old black man
begging for fifty cents
his tongue whapping
around, sliding out
the anti-psychotics
not right.

∞

if the mountain has no path
it may be the wrong mountain

the fool is king
of his mistakes
arrayed like an army
before him

∞

self pity gets a bad rap

∞

morality sucks immorality slurps.

∞

knew two men
who fought for patton.
one conservative
one communist
both passionate
both loved patton
both dealt with scoundrels

# About the Author

rd coleman was born in Hollywood, at Cedars of Lebanon Hospital. Still an infant, he returned to New York (having been conceived there) via Chicago, but once back in New York, pretty much stayed put. He grew up in Washington Heights, first going to a very small, local private school which only took him to the third grade. He did very well there and never should have left. He then went to PS 169, where, it was rumored, Abraham Lincoln spoke when in town seeking the Republican nomination for President. That year, Mr Lincoln also gave a speech at Cooper Union. History seeped into his bones. History always was one of his good subjects. He subsequently went to two junior high schools, at least three high schools, and settled down to a full four years at Hunter College, Bronx division (now Lehman College) because men were still not allowed downtown, to go to Marjorie Morningstar's school. At Hunter, his grade point averages generally remained one tenth of a percent above the expulsion point. After completing 27 credits towards a 30 credit Masters Degree, at San Francisco State College, he tossed it all away and returned to New York. Initially, he wanted to go to UC Berkeley and study Philosophy, that having been his major in undergraduate school, but he was told he would not fit in. He had not fitted in college, various high schools and junior highs, so he didn't see any problem. He never had a chance to prove that he would not fit in at Cal, too.

He has done some teaching; he has worked for the City's Department of Welfare; he has been a street worker with gangs on the lower east side, a union organizer and a union bureaucrat. He was a director of various homeless shelters and became a NYC commissioner before encountering an agency head who also believed he didn't fit in.

His first work was published in the mid-sixties.

# About NYQ Books™

NYQ Books™ was established in 2009 as an imprint of The New York Quarterly Foundation, Inc. Its mission is to augment the *New York Quarterly* poetry magazine by providing an additional venue for poets already published in the magazine. A lifelong dream of NYQ's founding editor, William Packard, NYQ Books™ has been made possible by both growing foundation support and new technology that was not available during William Packard's lifetime. We are proud to present these books to you and hope that you will continue to support The New York Quarterly Foundation, Inc. and our poets and that you will enjoy these other titles from NYQ Books™:

| | |
|---|---|
| Joanna Crispi | *Soldier in the Grass* |
| Ted Jonathan | *Bones and Jokes* |
| Amanda J. Bradley | *Hints and Allegations* |
| Ira Joe Fisher | *Songs from an Ealier Century* |
| Kevin Pilkington | *In the Eyes of a Dog* |

Please visit our website for these and other titles:

## www.nyqbooks.org